THE GOLDEN BLADE

TRUMPET TO THE MORN

2001

53rd   EDITION

Anthroposophy springs from the work and teaching of Rudolf Steiner. He described it as a path of knowledge, to guide the spiritual in the human being to the spiritual in the universe.

The aim of this annual journal is to bring the outlook of anthroposophy to bear on questions and activities   relevant to the present, in a way which may have lasting value. It was founded in 1949 by Charles Davy and Arnold Freeman, who were its first editors.

The title derives from an old Persian legend, according to which King Jamshid received from his god, Ahura Mazda, a golden blade with which to fulfil his mission on earth. It carried the heavenly forces of light into the darkness of earthly substance, thus allowing its transformation. The legend points to the possibility that humanity, through wise and compassionate work with the earth, can one day regain on a new level what was lost when the Age of Gold was supplanted by those of Silver, Bronze and Iron. Technology could serve this aim; instead of endangering our planet's life, it could help to make the earth a new sun.

TRUMPET TO THE MORN

Edited by William Forward and Simon Blaxland-de Lange

The Golden Blade

First published in 2000 by The Golden Blade
© 2000 The Golden Blade
The Golden Blade
Emerson College
Forest Row
East Sussex RH18 5JX
England

ISBN 0-9531600-3-3
ISSN 0967-6708

Printed in Great Britain
by Design To Print, Forest Row, East Sussex

Contents

Editorial Notes

It has been our policy over the last few years to identify a theme and then solicit articles from individuals who may have something interesting to say about it. In preparing for the present issue, however, we wanted to mark the first year which is firmly within the new millennium by, in effect, allowing the theme to be shaped by the contributions which came towards us. The only proviso made when requesting articles - and the endeavour was made to cast the net fairly widely throughout the anthroposophical movement - was that authors should focus in their respective fields of expertise upon ideas or initiatives with a particularly seminal quality for the century or millennium that is now beginning. We also hoped to encourage as many members as possible of the younger generation to contribute, on the grounds that is they who will be responsible for guiding the affairs of humanity over the coming decades. Ideally, the resulting contributions would reflect a total picture of the breadth of on-going research and initiative-taking within the compass of Anthroposophy, but inevitably there are many areas which are not represented. Readers are invited to enable these to find their voice for next year!

Out of the articles included in the present volume a distinct theme emerges. Without exception, our contributors have written out of a deep sense of urgency, an awareness that the dawning of this new millennium is a time pregnant with new possibilities but also burdened by the legacy of a century characterised by an unprecedented destructiveness - the consumption of natural resources accumulated over thousands or millions of years, the breakdown of the social forms and cultural perspectives inherited from the past, and the death of vast numbers of human beings through the agency of wars and other man-made catastrophes. Our title, "Trumpet to the Morn", evokes this mood of a new day emerging out of the night's gloom. The phrase is taken from the first scene of *Hamlet,* when the nocturnal visitations of the ghost of Hamlet's father have been abruptly terminated by the cock proclaiming the imminent rising of the Sun. There is at this moment - which is reflected in some lines of glorious poetry - a sense that the sinister shades of darkness have been banished by a light of greater power and certainty, a light which may be associated with the birth of the consciousness soul (it would be not inappropriate to interpret this scene as a dramatic rendering of this moment in human evolution).

But what exactly is heaving over the horizon at the dawning of the new millennium? With Hamlet the drama of freeing himself from the past still had to be played out, with tragic consequences for himself and those around him. Now that this legacy has been swept away it is as though we stand today at the same moment of dawning but with a power of choice which Shakespeare's tragic heroes did not have. If we have not gained the necessary self-knowledge and fail to free ourselves from our dependence on outward structures and securities, we shall see only the Prince of Darkness masquerading as the light of a New Age. Immense resources have been invested to ensure that this sense of servile dependency lives on in as many people as possible. Market-led globalisation - the dominant force at this millennium threshold - together with the competitive social Darwinism in every sphere of life which it engenders, is the shadow side of a Michaelic world economic brotherhood; and it fosters, and is held in place by, a deep unconsciousness in the realm of the will which breeds within the individual a sense of servility, powerlessness and irresponsibility. The context is thereby created for the kind of political master portrayed by Vladimir Solovyov in his "A Short Story of Antichrist",[1] who will make full use of, on the one hand, the growing tendency for people to communicate with electronic machines instead of with one another and, on the other, the rapid impoverishment of language itself - through which alone such communication can presently be conducted - by phenomena such as Political Correctness.

What is needed at this juncture is, however, not so much a litany of what is wrong with the world but an environment in which the considerable numbers of individuals who wish to welcome the dawning of the true Sun can work creatively together, thus fashioning an alternative world-picture to the currently dominant "global market-place/village". Fortunately, the basis for such an environment already exists in the form of the land, although the desperate state of modern agriculture speaks volumes for the extent to which the land, the physical basis for our lives on this Earth, is currently neglected. Take, for example, the plight of an actual young, hard-working Lakeland hill farmer and his wife, who live with their four young children in one of the many Lakeland valleys which man has beautified through his activities over recent centuries. Without the sheep the area would revert to impenetrable bracken and forest, and great tracts of the area would not only lose their present exquisite aesthetic balance but would become inaccessible to the many walkers who roam the fells. And yet the price that the farmer receives for the sheep's fleeces is so low that many of them - in particular the Herdwick breed, ideally suited to survival in the wet, chilly climate - are not worth taking to market and have to be

---

[1] This story concludes his book War, Progress and the End of History: Three Conversations (1900), published in English by Lindisfarne Press, 1990.

disposed of, generally by burning them. At sheep-shearing time, the farmer will devote days of twelve hours and more of devoted back-braking labour to a task which ends with the fruits of his work going up in smoke the following morning. There are contractors who will do the job, but they charge a not unreasonable sum of 50 pence per sheep - a lot of money to pay out if one is getting little or nothing for the fleece. Moreover, when he takes his sheep to market, he will be lucky if he receives any money for them at all from the auctioneer (the lambs are somewhat more profitable). In economic terms, the farmer's work is largely meaningless (although one could argue that it need not be so) and it is sustained largely by subsidy cheques coming through the letterbox. And yet - although some would disagree - in real terms it fulfils an important need. The most astonishing aspect of this scenario is that the average visitor to the Lake District is unaware that the agricultural activity which predominates in the area is from a certain point of view a meaningless charade. In contrast to the wealth of literature in local bookshops about the pleasures that are to be had from the various amenities offered by the area, one will literally find nothing about the bleak realities of its main current agricultural activity (and it is, after all, an agricultural area as opposed to an industrial centre).

Passing from this tiny vignette of one of England's most cherished natural sanctuaries back to the wider, global picture, the activities of Nicanor Perlas - himself a biodynamic farmer by profession - deserve a further mention (see the Editorial Notes of the *Golden Blade* for the year 2000). Nicanor Perlas is remarkable in managing to combine three elements which by no means often coincide. He is an anthroposophist who has a leading position in the Anthroposophical Society of the Philippines; but he also has very strong links with and sympathies for the "alternative movement". Most rarely, however, he has been involved in what would appear to be a highly successful approach to the political powers-that-be of his own country which is making an impact on the way that its affairs are conducted at a national level. Through Perlas's work in the Philippines (and doubtless these islands offer a more favoured environment for this than the citadels of the West), the spirit-bearing cultural sphere - the aspect of Rudolf Steiner's threefold picture which has long been absent from the exoteric landscape of modern society - becomes outwardly visible alongside the more generally recognised economic and rights spheres. In his book, *Shaping Globalisation: Civil Society, Cultural Power and Threefolding* (Centre of Alternative Development Initiatives, Philippines, 1999), he demonstrates that this realm where the individual thinking human spirit is sovereign has an absolutely crucial role to play if the 21st century is to witness the bright dawning heralded in Horatio's speech cited in our title. This quality is beautifully encapsulated in Corinna Gleide's short essay - published this year in *Das Goetheanum* as a Whitsun study - which serves as an introduction to the series of articles that follows.

We were pleased to agree to a request from several of our correspondents that we should publish a lecture by Rudolf Steiner in this new issue of the *Golden Blade*. In the lecture that we have chosen, which is, referred to by Sergei Prokofieff in his article as "The Imagination of Europe", Steiner sets the scene for our deliberations by surveying the modern age against the background of the most ancient history of mankind, as seen through the eyes of Greek creation mythology. He describes how in the European heartland of the post-Christian cultural development of mankind, a region extending eastward as far as the Ural mountains, an impenetrable wall arose during early Christian times from Earth to heaven which concealed from European humanity the now decadent traces of man's vision of the spiritual world, or the Pleroma as it was known in ancient Gnostic traditions. By the 20th century the brilliant Luciferic intellectuality of this Western (European) region and the debased magical arts deriving from the Ahrimanic corruption of the Pleroma in the East (Asia) had led to mankind being threatened by an immense danger originating from the astral sphere - the lowest region of the spiritual world, bordering on the earthly realm. Steiner indicates that the only way that human beings can overcome this danger is that they develop a clear understanding of what is going on in this astral sphere. He was speaking in 1923 specifically about the forces lurking behind Bolshevism, which had only latterly asserted its sovereignty in Russia. From the course which events took in the 20th century, it is evident that his warnings largely fell on deaf ears. But how may we in the year 2000 interpret his graphic picture of these decadent forces living in the astral world, with their power to allure human beings from the earthly sphere into their domain and obsessively rivet their attention to this seductive combination of intellectual brilliance and material desire? It is difficult not to make an association with the current fascination with Information Technology; and as one reads Steiner's description, images of cyberspace messages thronging super-earthly (or sub-earthly) highways may well come to mind. The article by Prokofieff on Bolshevism and its antecedents and ramifications, and that by Harlan Gilbert on computer technology develop certain essential aspects of the questions raised by Steiner; while Jonael Schickler's article on trends in modern philosophy and Bodo von Plato's essay on history and the study of history approach these two academic disciplines out of a commitment to develop the clear understanding which in his lecture Rudolf Steiner insists is so necessary if mankind is to avoid falling into illusion or despair.

This group of five articles is followed by a second group of three contributions, each of which focuses on a particular area in the light of the overall theme. Bernard Jarman chose to write about Seed Production as the most crucial area of research which the BDAA has to offer the world at the present time, and he indicates in his article the reasons of his choice. James Dyson's article, which is now being made available to a general readership, addresses the potential contribution of anthroposophical medicine to modern psychiatry; and Alex Naylor eloquently describes the vision lying behind his forthcoming major feature film - due for release in 2004 - on Lord Nelson and the Battle of Trafalgar. Two Book Reviews and a letter complete the volume. The Prokofieff book belongs more to the historical symptomatology of the first group of articles, while the volumes by Coenraad van Houten exemplify the anthroposophical research described in the second group. Finally we publish Angus Jenkinson's letter about Jostein Saether's work on karma research, because it creates a balance which we would have wished to achieve when publishing the article by the Norwegian doctors in this year's 2000 issue but were unable to for purely practical reasons.

Our acknowledgements go to all our contributors, correspondents and of course our readers, without whom there would be no *Golden Blade*. A special word of thanks goes to Anne Stockton, who for the third year in succession - and at an age when most people have opted for peaceful retirement - has designed our cover. We also wish to record our deep appreciation of Andrew Wolpert's contribution to the *Golden Blade* over the past ten years. Some readers will recall that he joined William Forward as co-editor shortly after Adam Bittleston died in May 1989. He has decided to relinquish his editorial responsibilities in order to be able to focus more on his other work, while retaining a keen interest in the magazine; and we shall greatly miss his verve, sparkling humour and his great ability to find the right turn of phrase for the situation.

In conclusion, we make no apology for raising the price of the *Golden Blade* from £7 to £8, on the grounds that we have held it at this level for the past seven years despite a steady increase in costs. Production of the magazine in this particular form would no longer be viable without this increase.

S. B-de L.
August 2000

Clairvoyance and Thinking

The Individualisation of Anthroposophy*

Corinna Gleide

Where are the Initiates?

It is often said that Anthroposophy needs to be individualised in individual human beings. Particularly since the personalities who had personally experienced Rudolf Steiner, or were pupils of such persons, have died. Thereby a certain spiritual stream, a stream of tradition, has become interrupted, or at least there is a caesura, and questions about the continuation or even renewal of Anthroposophy exercise many people today.

Friedrich Rittelmeyer once asked Rudolf Steiner: "Where are the 'Initiates of Mankind' today, when a work such as yours is at stake?' Rudolf Steiner answered: " Now it is imperative that the higher truths are grasped by human thinking. If you were to meet these initiates nowadays, you might not find in them what you are seeking. They had their tasks more in former incarnations. Now the thinking of mankind has to be spiritualised."

Here we have the juxtaposition: the initiate and human thinking. The higher worlds should be grasped through thinking, whereas the initiates had their task in former times. What one expects of them one might perhaps not find in them at all.

What do we then expect of the initiates? At the time when Rittelmeyer, in the years 1916-1918, regularly spoke with Rudolf Steiner, he was concerned that Steiner's work would urgently have needed greater support ("Where such a work as yours is at stake"), and the question which exercised him was whether the necessary support could not have come from initiates.

Rittelmeyer's question is still relevant today. Even today the question of new initiates in the anthroposophical movement is often asked. What is expected of the initiates today? I would say that one expects advice, answers, for example, to the question: how should we go on; what would

Translated by Carlotta Hollman-Dyson. Originally published in German in *Das Goetheanum* dated 4th June 200.

it be necessary to do? One also expects new revelations. One expects also above all a continuation of the School of Spiritual Science. Rudolf Steiner's answer to Rittelmeyer could not have been more explicit for the time then. The important thing is not an intervention "from above" but rather that the higher truths are grasped through thinking, that the thinking of the individual human being is spiritualised. One might add: that would have been the support which Rudolf Steiner would have needed.

Grey Theory, or Spiritualisation of Thinking?

What is our situation now with regard to the spiritualisation of thinking? It seems to me that for quite a while there has been an uncertainty in this regard in the different fields of anthroposophical work. I see particularly two directions in which the consequences of this uncertainty manifest themselves. The one consequence is that in the practical realms which originated as anthroposophical daughter movements it has become very difficult to maintain the connection with the spiritual world. In many places the activities have become detached.

A second consequence is that nowadays there are people who speak of their own spiritual experience and research without reference to the realm of ideas/thinking. Many listeners are seeking there a less "theoretical" meeting with the spiritual world.

One of the most outstanding qualities of Rudolf Steiner is, however, that he availed himself in a particular way of ideas and concepts to describe his spiritual perceptions in order to make clear to readers and listeners what he was talking about. It was most important to him to emphasize again and again that in this way the contents of spiritual science did not need to be believed but could become accessible to individual endeavour. Moreover, they should not just be accepted but be understood and examined. The presentation of spiritual realities in the form of ideas has thus become a methodical principle of anthroposophical presentations, as the new revelations are intended to stand in a different relationship to the individual than has ever previously been the case. One is to grasp and digest them in one's thinking, thus individualising them. Because autonomy can only come through thinking, Rudolf Steiner chose this route.

Now there is a core problem which is probably the main problem altogether when we are dealing with the formation of ideas and the spiritualisation of thinking. This problem is strongly connected with the intellectual, or mind soul, which is still working strongly both in society and civilisation as well as in the individual. This means that we cling instinctively to norms, blueprints, laws and constraints etc. We tend towards generalisations and towards turning what we have comprehended into a "thing out there." We still think and feel in hierarchical terms, which means that we do not take full responsibility for what is important to us. I also suspect that the desertion of practitioners has not so much to do with the ideas of Anthroposophy as with what the understanding intellect has made of them. This is - rightly - experienced as sterile and theoretical.

The same holds true nowadays for people who would rather not speak about, or listen to, spiritual experiences without regard to the realm of ideas. The spiritual experiences seem more real, more motivating and fulfilling than the apparently grey theories about the "sheaths" of the human being or the development of the earth from Old Saturn via Old Sun to Old Moon.

Individualisation of Cognition

In the Apocalypse of St. John, the angel, around whose head gleams the rainbow, whose countenance is like the sun and whose feet are like pillars of fire, gives John a book. The angel says to John: "Take this and eat it; it will be bitter in your stomach, although in your mouth it is as sweet as honey." John eats the book; in his mouth it is as sweet as honey, but when he has eaten it, his insides are filled with a bitter taste. This event refers to a point in the history of humanity at which we have now arrived. It is the point where the spiritual revelations, as written in the book, have to be eaten by the individual, where they have to permeate one completely, i.e., where one has to individualise them completely in oneself. But what does that mean? How can that happen?

The decisive point is that with Anthroposophy, the beginning of the individualisation process takes place in the pure thinking of the individual. It is important that the ideas of Anthroposophy are permeated as much as possible with pure thinking. The important thing is the power, the exertion of will with which we learn to maintain ourselves in pure thinking, for it is in this concentration of force that one can learn to experience/perceive one's own ego. It is at this point that one begins to experience the rudiments of the higher ego; here the ego is pure activity. Fichte called this experience, which leads to the awakening of the ego, the "deed-action."

The above is a relatively point-centred experience of one's own self, where the self is experienced as activity or like a centre of force, but lacking pictures. Through a study of the fundamental texts of spiritual science, a certain peripheral experience of the self can be added.

Through such intensive work in the realm of thinking, on spiritual-scientific cosmology and on the spiritual hierarchies, it may occur that in the course of time these conceptions begin to become pictorial and imbued with being-ness.

Besides pure thinking, feeling plays an important part here. With one's own thoughts, which have become clairvoyant, one begins to live in this being-imbued cosmos; and when one is doing this, one notices that in all this one's own higher being is living. Thus one meets oneself because one's own higher ego is involved in cosmic evolution, and with the spiritual beings who bring it about.

At this point the efforts to individualise thinking experience a breakthrough. Through my willed exertion of thinking, I have reached the point where the I generates and experiences itself in pure thought. In the second step, particularly through thinking imbued with feeling, I have begun to grasp with amazement how this ego lives in all that Steiner describes as the evolution of the earth through the work of the hierarchies. "The world is another form of the ego," says Christian Morgenstern. In human self-knowledge the spiritual being of the cosmos is revealed.

The Aristotelian-Platonic Organ of Perception

The two ego-experiences described above are clearly distinct from one another and yet belong inseparably together. In the pure thought-experience of the self the Aristotelian technique of conception and training of thinking live in a new form. In the self imaginative experience of the periphery, human thinking unites with its cosmic origins. Therein lies a new form of Platonism, a unification, in thought, with the cosmic-imaginative archetypes of the world. Neither of these ego experiences is attainable by an untrained thinking. Their linking together in this form represents something completely new in the spiritual evolution of humanity: the modern connection of the consciousness soul with the spiritual world. Never before in the history of human thinking has it been possible to individualise spiritual knowledge in this way. In every human being who treads this path an individualised cosmic spirit is born. Anthroposophy is then no longer just traditional book-knowledge, but one recognises it in the content of one's own cosmic spirit. In the place of dependency on Rudolf Steiner there arises the feeling of being able to work independently for the same cause as he, and - despite the huge difference in capacities - to be standing on the same level with him in principle.

In this way there arises in the individual an "ideal" organ of cognition, the organ of cognitive clairvoyance, which has its home exactly on the boundary between sensory and spiritual reality. The spiritual self is open "downwards" towards the physical and "upwards" towards the spiritual. From this point, one can get some sense of the limited value of clairvoyance which is not carried by ideas which have been elaborated by the individual concerned. This kind of clairvoyance cannot be mediated to sensory reality in a harmonious way. It also becomes clear that practical activities are bound to become increasingly and one-sidedly determined by the "compelling realities" of the sense world, if the people engaged in them do not develop the organ described above. For without the bridging function of this organ the spiritual world can find no real entry into daily life and action.

Only a clairvoyant thinking, born out of the connection between Platonism and Aristotelianism in a new form, as the central anthroposophical organ of perception, is capable of building the bridge between the sense world and the spiritual world.

Therefore I believe that the further development of Anthroposophy in our time does not depend only or primarily on the activity of a new initiate, but on consistent individualisation in the thinking of each person. This alone would be a precondition and a starting point for a future form of co-operation with an initiate teacher.

The mysteries of the Pleroma:
the corruption of their influences in Europe and Asia today

Rudolf Steiner

In a time of great and momentous decisions such as the present it is all the more necessary that in their study of contemporary events and happenings, men's minds should also be raised to the spirit The spirit is no abstraction but a reality which transcends and works into the physical life of humanity. It is by no means enough to admit that the spirit pervades all things physical, for this is to recognise one fragment only of the world in which man lives and moves as a thinking and acting being. For many centuries it was justifiable to hold such a view, but in our age this justification has ceased. In the lecture today, therefore,, we will consider how certain happenings in the physical world are connected with impulses emanating from the spiritual world.

To begin with, we will study the character of certain spiritual impulses which have been at work in the course of evolution and have led on to the present state of affairs in the world. For long ages now, Western civilisation and its offshoots have paid attention to one fragment only of the whole story of the evolution of the world, and from a certain point of view this was quite right. In times when the Old Testament became the authoritative record, it was proper to regard the creation of man by Jahve or Jehovah as the dawn of world evolution.

But in still earlier times the intervention of Jehovah was regarded not as the incipient but as a much *later* episode in the evolutionary process. It was said that another, more purely spiritual phase of evolution had preceded

Lecture given in Dornach, 15th July, 1923. The original German text is contained in the volume entitled *Kulturphanomene-Drei Perspektiven der Anthroposophie* (No. 225 in the Bibliographical Survey, 1961, of the Complete Edition of Rudolf Steiner's works.) Published by permission of the Rudolf Steiner Nachlassverwaltung, Dornach, Switzerland. Published in 1931 in *Anthroposophy,* No. 3, Vol. 6, under the title "Gnostic Doctrines and Supersensible Influences in Europe".
*When this translation was made in 1931, the word "men" would have been understood to mean human beings in general. Although we are aware that this word has now contracted in its meaning, we have chosen not to alter the original translation.

the creation of the world by Jehovah as it is described in the Bible and as it is ordinarily understood. In other words, it was held that the intervention of Jehovah had been preceded by that of other Beings, that the creation of man had occurred after the passage of an earlier phase of the evolutionary process.

Those men in Greece who meditated upon the earliest stages of world-evolution spoke of a primordial Being for the understanding of whose nature a much more highly spiritual mode of knowledge is required than for an understanding of the events described in the Old Testament. These men spoke of the Being whom they held to be the actual Creator of the world - the Demiurgos.

The Demiurgos was a Being dwelling in spheres of lofty spirituality, in a world devoid of every element of that material existence with which the Bible story the humanity created by Jehovah is naturally associated.

We must therefore think of the Demiurgos as a sublime Being, as the Creator of the world who sends forth other Beings from Himself. The Beings sent forth by the Demiurgos were ranked in successive stages, each stage being lower than the last. (Such expressions are, of course, quite inadequate, but no other words are available.) The life of these Beings, however, was held to be entirely free from the conditions of earthly birth and earthly death.

In Greece they were known as Æons - of the first rank, the second rank and so on. The Æons were Beings who had issued from the Demiurgos. Among these Æons, Jahve or Jehovah was a Being of a relatively subordinate rank. And this brings us to a consideration of the teachings of the Gnostics, as they were called, in the early centuries of Christendom. It was said that Jehovah united with matter and that from this union *man* came into existence.

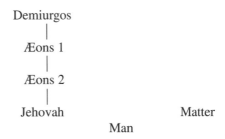

According to this Gnostic conception, therefore, Jehovah was a somewhat lower descendant of the lofty Æons who had proceeded from the Demiurgos, and as the outcome of Jehovah's union with matter, man was created.

"Pleroma" was the name given to a world which transcends, although it has its basis in, the phenomena of the world of sense. This conception was thoroughly unintelligible to the Ancients although it was utterly beyond the grasp of a later humanity. The Pleroma was a world at a higher level than the physical world but peopled none the less by individualised Beings. And at the lowest level, at the lowest stage of the Pleroma, the human being created by Jehovah comes into existence. At this same stage, another Being appears, a Being incorporate not in the individual man nor yet in a nation, but rather in humanity taken as one whole, a Being who remembers its descent from the Demiurgos and strives again to reach the spiritual world. The name of this Being was Achamoth and in Greece, *Achamoth* was a personification of the spiritual strivings of mankind. The urge which lives in men to reach the spiritual world again was therefore said to be due to Achamoth.

Another conception was then added to this world of ideas, namely, that in order to reward the strivings of Achamoth, the Demiurgos sent down an Æon of a very high rank. This Æon - so it was said - united with the man Jesus in order that the strivings of Achamoth might be fulfilled. The Gnostic teaching was that in the man Jesus there had dwelt a Being belonging to the ranks of the Æons, a Being of a far higher spiritual order than Jahve or Jehovah.

And so, among those in whom these ideas lived during the early Christian centuries - and the hearts of many men in those times were turned with the deepest fervour and reverence to the mystery of Golgotha - there grew up the conception of the great mystery connected with the man Jesus in whom a holy Æon had come to dwell.

Study of this mystery took many different forms but no essential purpose would be served today by entering into a detailed consideration of the various ideas current in Greece, Asia Minor and its neighbouring districts, as to the manner in which this Æon had been incorporate in the man Jesus. The kind of ideas which in those days men brought to their study of a mystery of this character have long since passed away from the sphere of human thinking. Man's thought today is concerned with all that surrounds and is connected with his life between birth and death and at best there dawns upon him the realisation that spiritual foundations underlie this physical world of sense. Direct, inner experience of the kinship of the human soul with the Pleroma which was once a matter of immediate experience and referred to as naturally as we refer today to man's connection with the spiritual world - which was moreover of far greater interest to human beings in those days than the physical world - this too has passed away. There is no longer any direct experience of kinship with the spiritual world. Such ideas lived in European civilisation no longer than the first three, or rather no longer than the first three and greater part of the fourth centuries of our era. By that time the minds of men were no longer capable of rising to the sphere known as the Pleroma, and the dawn of another age had broken. Among the first thinkers of this age were Augustine and Scotus Erigena. It was the age of Scholasticism, and of European Mysticism at its prime, an epoch when the language of the mind bore little resemblance to the language used in the early days of Christendom. Men's minds were now directed to the physical world of sense and on the basis of this material world they endeavoured to evolve their concepts and ideas of the supersensible world.

Direct experience of kinship with the spiritual world, with the Pleroma, had died away. The time had come for man to pass into an entirely different phase of development. It is not a question here of the respective merits of two epochs of time, or of forming an opinion of the inherent value of the medieval mind. The point is to realise and understand that civilised humanity is faced with different tasks during the different epochs. In an earlier age, kinship with the world known as the Pleroma was a ,matter of immediate experience, and it was man's task and function to activate the spiritual forces of knowledge in the innermost recesses of the soul - the forces of spiritual aspiration. But as time went on, darkness crept over the world of the Pleroma. Faculties of an entirely different character began to function in the human mind and the development of rationalistic thought began. In the ages where there had been direct experience of kinship with the Pleroma, the faculty of individual thinking had not begun to function in the mind of man. Knowledge came to him through illumination, through inspiration and through an instinctive realisation of the supersensible world. His thoughts were revealed to him. The springing-forth of individual thoughts and the building of logical connections in thinking denoted a later phase, the coming of which was already foreshadowed by Aristotle. This later phase of evolution cannot really be said to have begun in any real sense before the second half of the fourth century of our era. By the time of the Middle Ages the energies of the human mind were directed wholly to the development of thought per se and of everything that is associated with the activity of thinking.

In this connection, medieval culture and, above all, Scholasticism, rendered inestimable service to the progress of civilisation. The faculty of thinking was turned to practical application in the shaping and association of ideas. A technique of thought of the very purest kind was worked out, although it too has been wholly lost.*

* See The Redemption of Thinking. Lectures by Rudolf Steiner on the philosophy of Thomas Aquinas

The re-acquisition of the technique of Scholastic thought is a goal to which humanity ought for their own sake to aspire. But it goes against the grain in our days, when men prefer to receive knowledge passively, not by dint of their own inner activity. The urge to inner activity is lacking in our present age, whereas in Scholasticism it lived and worked with a tremendous power. And that is why even today it is possible for the thought of men who understand the essence of Scholasticism to be far more profound, far more consistent than the thought emanating from the world of science. Modern scientific thought is formal, short-winded, often inconsistent. Men should really learn a lesson from the technique of Scholastic thought, but the learning will not be of the kind that finds favour today. It must be an active learning, not a learning that consists merely in assimilating knowledge that has already been laid down as a model, or deduced from experiments.

The Middle Ages, then, were the period during which man was meant to unfold an inner faculty in his soul, namely the faculty of thinking. The Gods drew a veil over the Pleroma - which was a direct revelation of their life and being - because, if this revelation had continued to influence the human mind, men would not have unfolded that strong, inner activity of thinking which came to the fore during the Middle Ages and from which sprang the new mathematics and its kindred sciences, all of which are the legacy of Scholasticism.

Let us try now to summarise what has been said. Throughout many centuries the Pleroma was a revelation vouchsafed to man. Through an act of Grace from on high, this world of light revealed itself in and through the light that filled the mind of man. A veil was then drawn over this world of light. Yonder in Asia, decadent remains of the world behind this veil were still preserved, but in Europe it was as though a precipitous wall arose from Earth to Heaven, a wall whose foundations stretched across the districts of the Ural Mountains and Volga, over the Black Sea and towards the Mediterranean. Try to picture to yourselves this great wall which grew up in Europe in consequence of the trend of evolution of which I have told you. It was an impenetrable wall, concealing from men all traces even of those decadent remains of an earlier vision of the Pleroma which were still preserved over in Asia. In Europe, this vision was completely lost. It was replaced by a technique of thinking from which a vista of the spiritual world was entirely absent. There you have a picture of the origin and subsequent development of medieval thought. Great though its achievements were, men's eyes were blinded to all that lay concealed behind the wall stretching from the Ural and Volga districts, over the Black Sea to the Mediterranean. Medieval thought was incapable of piercing this wall and though men hankered after the East, the East was no reality.

This is not a symbolic but a true picture of Europe as it was in the Middle Ages. Under the influences of a Giordano Bruno, a Copernicus, a Galileo, men felt the call to set about understanding the Earth beneath their feet. And they then proceeded to work out a science of the Heavens modelled upon their conception of the Earth, in contrast to the older science of the Earth which had been a reflection of heavenly love and of the mysteries of the Pleroma.

And so in the darkness there arose a new mode of knowledge and a new mental life, for the light was now shut off by the wall of which I have spoken.

The course of evolution is such that when the time is ripe for the development of certain definite faculties in one portion of the human race, other portions of humanity are separated off as it were behind a veil. And in the case of which we are speaking, a decadent culture grew up in the East behind the wall which had now been erected on the Earth, while Europe saw the beginnings of what was later to develop into Western culture in its most characteristic form. As a matter of fact the position today is fundamentally the same, except that men try now by means of historical records and an external mode of knowledge devoid of all insight into the mysteries of the Pleroma, to inform themselves about the dark secrets of existence. The significance of these things in the present age becomes quite apparent when we look over to the East, behind the great wall, where decadence has corrupted an earlier insight into the world known as the Pleroma. What was once an instinctive but at the same time a highly spiritual form of knowledge has become corrupt; the life of the human soul in the spiritual worlds has descended to the material world which from the Middle Ages onwards was the only world that remained accessible to the mind of man. Over yonder in the East we see a culture which in the true sense is not culture at all but an impulse to give an earthly, physical garb to purely *spiritual* experiences awakened by insight into the mysteries of the Pleroma.

Deeds of the Gods in the world of the Gods were conceived as the deeds of idols and the worship of idols superseded the worship of the Gods. Forces belonging in truth to the world of the Pleroma were dragged down to the material realm, and gave rise to the practice of corrupt magical arts in the regions of Northern Asia. The magic arts practised by the Shamanic peoples of Northern Asia and their aftermath in Central Asia (Southern Asia too was affected to a certain extent but remained somewhat freer), are an example of the corrupt application of what had once been a direct vision of the Pleroma. What ought to have been achieved, and in earlier times was achieved by the inner activity of the soul was now assisted by earthly magic. The forces living in the Pleroma were dragged down to the material world in an Ahrimanic form and were applied not only on Earth but in the spiritual world bordering on the Earth, the influences of which pour down upon human beings. And so, eastward of the Ural and Volga regions, in the astral world which borders on our physical world, there arose during the later Middle Ages, continuing through the centuries to our own day, an Ahrimanic form of magic practised by certain spiritual beings who in their etheric and astral development stand higher than man but in their development of soul and spirit stand lower than man. Throughout the regions of Siberia and Central Asia, in the spiritual world immediately adjacent to the earthly world, terrible etheric-astral beings are to be seen, Ahrimanic beings who practise an earthly, materialised form of magic. And these forces work upon human beings who are unskilled in such arts but who are infected by them and so come under the influence of this astral world.

In connection with these matters we must remember that ancient mythological lore was the outcome of a wonderfully spiritual conception of Nature. When men spoke in Greece of the fauns and satyrs and of the activities of the fauns and satyrs in earthly happenings, these beings were not the creation of fantasy as modern scholars would have us believe. The Greeks knew the reality of the fauns and satyrs who peopled the astral sphere adjacent to the earthly world. Approximately at the turn of the third and fourth centuries of our era these astral beings withdrew into regions lying eastwards of the Ural, the Volga and the Caucasus. This territory became their home and there they entered upon their later phase of development.

Against this cosmic background the faculty of thought in its pure form began to evolve in the souls of the men of Europe. So long as they adhered rigidly to an inwardly pure, inwardly austere activity of thinking of which Scholasticism affords a splendid example, their development was thoroughly in harmony with the aims of the spiritual world. They were preparing for something that must be achieved in our present age and in the immediate future. But this purity was not everywhere maintained. Eastwards of the great wall of which I have spoken, the urge had arisen to drag down the forces of the Pleroma to the earthly world and apply them in an earthly, Ahrimanic form of magic. And westwards of this wall, the urge towards rationalistic thought and towards a purely intellectual grasp of the earthly world mingled with the element of delight in material existence. In other words a Luciferic impulse gradually insinuated itself into the working of the faculty of pure reason now dawning in the human mind.

The result of this was the development of another astral world, immediately adjacent to the Earth, together with the efforts that were being made to unfold the faculties of pure reason and a pure, inwardly active form of thought. This astral world was ever-present among those who strove with the purity of purpose of men like Giordano Bruno, Galileo and others to promote the development of the faculty of earthly thought and to establish a standard and technique of thought. In and among all this activity we can divine the presence of beings belonging to an astral world - beings who attracted not only to themselves but to the religious life of men, forces proceeding from the element of delight in earthly existence, and whose aim was to bring the strivings for rationalistic thought into line with their own purposes. And so the efforts of the human mind to unfold the faculty of pure thought were gradually tinged with earthly, material considerations.

The technique of thought manifest in the latter part of the eighteenth century and especially in the nineteenth century was influenced in a very high degree by the astral forces which by this time had insinuated themselves into the sphere of rationalistic thought. The material desires of human beings which a pure and developed technique of thought ought to have been capable of clarifying and to some extent dispersing, gave birth to an element well-fitted to provide nourishment for certain astral beings who set out to direct the forces of this astute, keen thinking to the needs of material existence.

Such is the origin of systems of thought of which Marxism is an example. Instead of being sublimated to the realm of the spirit, thought was applied merely to the purposes of physical existence and of the world of sense. In this way the realm of human thinking became easy of access to certain Luciferic beings indwelling the astral world. The thoughts of men were impregnated through and through with the thoughts of these astral beings by whom the Western world was obsessed just as the East was now obsessed by astral beings whose existence had been made possible by the decadent magic arts practised among the Shamanic peoples. Under the influence of these astral beings, the element of earthly craving and desire crept into the realm of an astute but at the same time material mode of thought. And from this astral world influences played into and took possession of men of the type of Lenin and his contemporaries.

We have therefore to think of two worlds: one lying eastwards of the districts of the Ural Mountains, the Volga and the Caucasus, and the other westwards of this region. These two worlds in themselves constitute one astral sphere. The beings of this astral region are striving in our present age to enter into a kind of cosmic union. Westwards of the Ural and Volga districts live the beings whose life-breath is provided by the thinking of the West, permeated as it is by a Luciferic influence. In the astral sphere eastwards of the Ural and Volga districts dwell those beings whose life-element is provided by magic arts which are the debased, materialised form of what once was a power functioning in the world known as the Pleroma. These beings are striving to unite, with the result that there has come into existence an astral region in which human beings are involved, and which they must learn to understand. If they succeed in this, a task of first importance for the evolutionary progress of mankind will be accomplished. But if they persist in ignoring what is happening here, their inner life will be taken hold of by the fiery forces emanating from the Ahrimanic beings of Asia and the Luciferic beings of Europe as they strive to consummate their cosmic union. Human beings are in danger of becoming obsessed by these terrible forces emanating from the astral world. Eastwards and westwards of the Ural and Volga districts, then, we must conceive of the existence of an astral region immediately adjacent to the Earth - a region which is the earthly dwelling place of beings who are the fauns and satyrs in a later metamorphosis.

If the *whole* reality is revealed to us as we look over towards the East of Europe today, we see not human beings alone, but an astral sphere which since the Middle Ages has become the Paradise of beings once known as the fauns and satyrs. And if we understand the nature of these beings, we can also follow the processes of metamorphosis through which they have passed since then. These beings move about among men and carry on their activities in the astral world, using on the one hand the Ahrimanic forces of decadent, Eastern magic and on the other, the forces emanating from the Luciferic, rationalistic thinking of the West. And human beings on the Earth are influenced and affected by these forces.

In their present state, the goat-form which constitutes the lower part of the bodily structure of these beings has coarsened and become bear-like, but on the other hand their *heads* are radiant and possessed of a high order of intelligence. They are the mirrored personifications of Luciferic rationalism developed to its highest point of subtlety. The beings indwelling this astral Paradise are half bear-, half goat-like in form, with semi-human countenances exhibiting a subtle sensuousness but at the same time a rare cleverness. Since the later Middle Ages and on through the centuries of the modern age this astral region has become a veritable Paradise of the satyrs and fauns in their present metamorphosis, and there they dwell.

And in the midst of all these mysterious happenings a laggard humanity goes its way, concerning itself merely with physical affairs. But all the time these forces - which are no less real than the phenomena of the world man perceives with his physical eyes and grasps with his physical brain - are playing into earthly existence.

The conditions now developing as between Asia and Europe cannot be fully intelligible until we understand them in their astral aspect, their spiritual aspect. The decadent forces emanating from Shamanic arts which have been preserved in the astral regions of Central and Northern Asia are striving to consummate a kind of cosmic union with the impulse which has received the name of Bolshevism, and eastwards and westwards of the Ural and Volga districts endeavours are being made to consummate a union between a certain form of magic and Bolshevism. It is a world of myth and is for this reason well-nigh incomprehensible to the modern mind. Luciferic elements in the form of Bolshevism are striving to unite with the decadent forces proceeding from Shamanic arts and coming over from the East. From West to East and from East to West forces are working and weaving in this astral Paradise. And the influences which pour down from this astral world into the earthly world emanate from the passionate efforts for union between the beings known in olden times as fauns and satyrs who surge over from the East, and the spirits of the West who have developed in a high degree everything that is connected with the head.

The spectacle presented to supersensible sight may be described in the following way: The nearer we come to the Ural and Volga districts, the more do these cloudlike, spiritual forms seem to gather together into a mass of heads, while the other parts of the bodily structure become indistinct. Seething over from the East we see those other beings, known in days of yore as the fauns and satyrs. Their once goat-like form has coarsened to a bear-like form and the further West they come in their efforts to consummate their astral union with the Luciferic beings of the West, the more do their heads seem to disappear. These beings come into existence in the astral world and the Earth-sphere is their home just as it is the home of physical humanity. They are the tempters and seducers of humanity on Earth because they can take possession of men; they can obsess human beings without in any way needing to convince them by means of speech.

It is urgently necessary that these things should be realised today. Men must awaken those inner faculties of soul which once gave birth to the mythological lore of olden times,. For it is only by rising to the sphere of Imaginative knowledge that we can stand with full consciousness in the onward-flowing stream of human evolution.

Bolshevism as an Initiation-Principle of Evil[1]

Sergei Prokofieff

As one looks back over the 20th century and contemplates the various forms of evil which have manifested themselves amongst mankind during its course, one's mind is arrested by the phenomenon of Bolshevism and by the need to understand it not only from an outward, political aspect but also from an occult standpoint. For in this century now coming to an end it is Bolshevism which - alongside National Socialism in Germany - stands out as having brought suffering on an almost inconceivable scale and death to vast numbers of people. For this reason it can be reckoned to be one of the mightiest manifestations of evil in the 20th century.

In what follows, however, Bolshevism shall be considered not as an outwardly historical phenomenon but as an impulse of evil which enters our world from a metahistorical domain (from a realm beyond history), as a spiritual impulse with the task of opposing the rightful course of human evolution. If we trace it back to its historical sources with the help of spiritual science, we reach the 7th century AD, or to be more precise, that particular year which corresponds to the number designated in the Revelation of St. John as the "number of the beast" (ch. 13:18).

Of course, such a way of approaching its origins would seem strange to anyone today outside anthroposophical circles. The reason for this is that the connection of Bolshevism - as the most significant phenomenon of evil in our time - with the 7th century AD cannot be discerned without the help of the results of Rudolf Steiner's spiritual-scientific research. However, once they been arrived at, these results are able to serve as a foundation for further research in this area which can shed an altogether new light also upon a 20th century phenomenon such as Bolshevism.

[1] Translated by S B-de L from a free - and considerably expanded - Russian version written by the author of a lecture that he gave in German in Boll (Germany) on 10th March 1999 and published in *Das Goetheanum*, no. 47 (21st November 1999), in a series of articles by various authors under the general title, "In the face of Evil in the 20th Century". A further development of the theme touched upon in the present article can be found in other books by the same author: *The Spiritual Origins of Eastern Europe and the Future Mysteries of the Holy Grail* (Temple Lodge 1993) and *The Encounter with Evil and its Overcoming through Spiritual Science* (Temple Lodge 1999).

An occult understanding of this phenomenon is of particular necessity at the present time, because the outward collapse of the Bolshevik regime in Russia has not by any means led to the disappearance of the deep forces which have nourished it from the historical scene. We should at this point think not only of China and North Korea but also of the many countries in the Third World where there are active political parties which formerly regarded Marxism and Bolshevism (Leninism) as wholly possible alternatives for the future evolution of humanity. Despite the enormity of the experience of actual Bolshevism in the 20th century, this conviction continues to exist both in Russia itself and in a number of other countries. Moreover, the phenomenon of Bolshevism can also be discerned in other current events of modern times where it would not outwardly seem to be in evidence but where it nevertheless continues to work beneath the surface as a mysterious guiding force. The tragedies in the Balkans and in Chechnya are only some of such examples in recent times.

On the other hand, if Bolshevism - as the most destructive manifestation of evil in the 20th century - is eventually to be overcome, the first step towards this from a spiritual-scientific point of view is that it is spiritually understood. For a start towards overcoming it can be made only within a human soul that is aspiring towards true self-knowledge. Only someone who has fully overcome its forces within his own soul will never succumb to its influence, in whatever veiled and hidden forms it may appear in our time or in the future. Furthermore, such a person will be able without fail to distinguish what really lies at the root of even the most complex historical situation - the poisonous effusions of that same archetypal phenomenon of evil which appeared in the 20th century in the form of Bolshevism. For in its primordial essence, evil is not part of the natural world surrounding a human being, or of the social environment with which he is connected, but a phenomenon which has its origin in the human soul itself and, from this source, enters into everything else, into the social and natural world. This is why a real understanding of the phenomenon of evil manifested in historical Bolshevism is possible only with the help of modern spiritual science, which makes it possible to discern in it four different levels or aspects; and only if these are examined as a totality can we be enabled to come closer to a true revelation of its historical and metahistorical sources.

The first of these levels is the historical one; the second is where the occult-political interests of certain secret brotherhoods of the West (the English-speaking countries) appear on the outward historical scene, especially immediately before and during the First World War. The third level, which can be described as the metahistorical, connects the phenomenon of Bolshevism with important spiritual events in the 7th century AD. Finally, the fourth level reveals the mystery of the activity in the phenomenon of Bolshevism itself of certain demonic beings of the supersensible world who are making every possible effort to oppose the rightful path of human evolution.

The First Level: The Historical Development of Bolshevism

The historical development of Bolshevism in Russia is directly associated with the tragedy of the First World War, which became the source of almost all the principal misfortunes of humanity in the 20th century. Thus Rudolf Steiner made considerable efforts to discover its causes, and on many occasions he described in detail in his lectures those events which were its source. In the present context, we cannot concern ourselves with all the vast material which Rudolf Steiner presented in this connection. Suffice it to say that the many historical facts and documents which he has cited, when combined with a right understanding of them on the foundation of spiritual science, throw an altogether new light upon everything that took place, to the extent that even generally familiar events are presented in a wholly different aspect from the official historical accounts even up to our own time.[1]

At the beginning of the 20th century there were in particular two powers that wanted a major war in Europe. In the first place, France, which after its defeat in the war with Germany in 1870-1871 (an event which led to the arising of the German Empire of the Kaisers) hungered for revenge and - above all - for the annexation of its former territory of Alsace-Lorraine. The second such power was Russia, where there was a strong warlike party which had arisen out of the Pan-Slavic stream, whose foundation lay in a document with a mysterious origin which subsequently became known as the pseudo-Testament of Peter the Great.[2] The members of this party had the aim of doing everything they could to establish in South-East Europe a confederation of the Eastern and Southern Slavic peoples in order to set it in opposition to the rest of Europe. These aims were, however, obstructed by the existence of the Austro-Hungarian Empire, which, therefore, needed to fall in order that the Slavic nations of the Danube Monarchy which belonged to it and those which were under its influence might join in a Pan-Slavic union under the leadership of Russia.

A third European power which played a decisive part immediately before the world war was Britain, a country which at the time had an immense influence upon all political relationships in Europe and, above all, upon whether peace or war would prevail. For Britain was in a position to prevent the war, but for various political reasons it did not want to do so.[3] And finally, at the centre of Europe there was the German Empire, which was in constant fear of being squeezed in pincers and, hence, of being forced to wage war on two fronts at once, both East and West. This was the military and political situation in Europe on the eve of the First World War.

Before this - in 1895 - Helmuth von Moltke appeared at the tsar's palace in St. Petersburg as an envoy of the German Kaiser. His task was to give the Russian Emperor a picture, beneath which was the inscription: "Nations of Europe, preserve your sacred property". This picture portrayed the souls of the various peoples of Christian Europe gathered under the sign of the Cross in the form of powerful maidens dressed in armour and armed with swords. They were united under the leadership of the Archangel Michael against a Sino-Mongolian danger approaching from the East, which was represented in the form of a figure sitting motionlessly on the clouds in a lotus position, with burning and destroyed European cities beneath it. This picture presented an altogether different vision of the combined activity of the Christian nations of Europe from what was manifested in August 1914.[4]

As has already been mentioned, an active war party had gradually formed in Russia out of the Pan-Slavic movement[5] which was working consciously towards the outbreak of war in Europe. In order to achieve their aim, the members of this party endeavoured to exert an increasing political and moral pressure upon the weak-willed tsar. However, in the immediate entourage of Nicholas II there was at that time a personality who, because of his influence on the tsar, to an increasing degree opposed their plans. This was Rasputin. There is no space here to give a more detailed charaterisation of this highly dubious figure. It is merely necessary to point out two of his characteristics: his unquestioning devotion to the tsar and his clairvoyant faculties, albeit of an atavistic nature. These faculties enabled Rasputin to determine without fail who in Nicholas II's immediate surroundings was really faithful to him and who was not. This also strongly coloured the advice which he gave the tsar in recommending people for particular government posts who would often - as regards their abilities - be altogether unsuitable for them. But Rasputin was guided in this respect by a completely different criterion - their inner faithfulness to the tsar. If this is not taken into consideration, the appointments made by the tsar on Rasputin's advice appear from an outward point of view completely meaningless and even harmful, as is generally stated by the majority of historians, who write only about his negative influence upon government affairs. Nevertheless, Rasputin was profoundly right in the sense that, in Nicholas's immediate surroundings there really were many individuals - especially amongst the adherents of the war party - who were unfaithful to him, for there were members of the French Masonic Lodge "Grand Orient de France" who, in accordance with their masonic oath, were obliged to represent the interests of France and place them above those of Russia. For people such as these, Rasputin represented a significant obstacle; and they therefore shortly afterwards made a first attempt on his life.[6] In order to recover from his wounds, Rasputin - who remained alive only by a miracle - was forced to return temporarily to his native village in the north of Russia.

At this time France announced a general mobilisation, and the Pan-Slavic party, making use of this situation and of the absence of Rasputin from the court, began to demand from the tsar that he proclaim a general mobilisation also in Russia. The tragic events in the Balkans gave very favourable grounds for this. And as soon as this happened, there immediately arose in Europe that situation which from the very beginning Germany had most dreaded as a nightmarish dream ; war on two fronts. As a result, it likewise rapidly brought about a general mobilisation. War in Europe was henceforth inevitable.

When Rasputin learnt from the north of Russia about Nicholas II's new order (general mobilisation), he sent him his famous letter. In this letter he referred to the war with Germany as the greatest misfortune which could befall Russia, and he went on to give a detailed description of his clairvoyant experience of the future Russia drowning in a sea of blood.[7] If one reads this letter today, one has the clear impression that what was revealed to its author in his prophetic vision were not so much the horrors and calamities of the First World War as the horrors and calamities of the Bolshevik Revolution and the subsequent Red Terror, which greatly exceeded the former in their magnitude.

Thus the war party achieved its purpose. As a result of the military events and the political crisis in Russia which they brought about, the Russian emperor was forced to abdicate from the throne, thus opening up this party's path to power.

Nevertheless - despite some initial successes - the situation on the Russo-German front had by 1917 reached total deadlock. In many places, military activity had ground to a halt. Russian and German soldiers were throwing down their weapons and openly fraternising with one another, for they could see no sense in this fratricidal war. At this time the only sensible political step for Russia was speedily to conclude a separate peace with Germany. This was in accord with its true and - one could say - vital interests. However, this did not occur. The reason was that, as has been pointed out, the overwhelming majority of the adherents of the war party which had come to power (the so-called "Provisional Government") were members of the lodge already referred to, the "Grand Orient de France"; and when they had been received into this lodge they had sworn to place the interests of France above all else. In France the greatest fear was of a separate peace between Russia and Germany, inasmuch as in this case Germany could transfer its Eastern army to the Western front and thus pose a military threat to Paris itself; and this was not to happen, come what may. As a result, contrary to all the true interests of Russia, the wholly meaningless war with Germany was continued "to the bitter end". By this means the new Russian government - in trying by whatever means to continue the war - quite literally betrayed Russia.

However, this artificial continuation of the war by whatever means soon brought about a quite particular political situation in Russia itself. For the general longing of the Russian people for peace was increasingly supplemented by the hopes of the peasantry - which at that time formed the majority of the population of the country - for an all-embracing land reform immediately after the end of the war. (Such a reform had already been discussed in the duma before the war, at the suggestion of one of the centre parties.)

In this mood of general expectations and hopes, the words "peace" and "land" were able to exert a truly magical, alluring effect upon great numbers of Russian people. The Bolsheviks did not fail to make immediate use of this state of affairs, and from the very start they placed these two magic words at the centre of their propaganda. However, on their lips they became no more than cheap, propagandist slogans. For when they spoke of "peace", the Bolsheviks had in mind an even more bloody civil war and the subsequent Red Terror, while in speaking of "land" they envisaged a "warlike communism" which brought about an unprecedented famine in the south of Russia, followed by the annihilation of the Russian peasantry, the large part of which was simply exterminated, and the rest forcibly herded into collective and State farms. Such were the actual consequences of the "land and peace" promised to the Russian people by the Bolsheviks.

One can therefore say that the Bolsheviks were by a devilish feat of genius able to make use of the dire political crisis which the world war brought about in Russia. For without the war Lenin and his followers would never have been able to seize power. Thus Rudolf Steiner was profoundly right in referring to the Bolsheviks as the legacy of that greatest of European tragedies - the First World War.

The Second Level: The Interests of the Secret Brotherhoods of the West behind the scenes of the First World War

In lectures which he gave during the First World War, Rudolf Steiner referred on a number of occasions to the particular occult-political interests of certain secret brotherhoods of the English-speaking West.[8] The direction of their interests is confirmed by a map of Europe published in England in the 1880s, to which Rudolf Steiner referred on more than one occasion. On this map Europe was portrayed in approximately the way that it actually became as a result of the First World War.[9] Directly across the territory of Russia was written the word "desert", a place for future social experiments.

A sufficient quantity of research has been published today to give documentary proof that the Bolshevik Revolution was brought about with the money of Western financiers, especially American and British, without whose financial assistance the implementation of the socialist experiment in Russia would hardly have been possible.[10]

Anyone who grew up in the Soviet Union had to familiarise himself with the Communist Party text-book on history. From this book he might learn not without surprise that soon after they came to power the "noble and honest" Bolsheviks, under Lenin's leadership, returned a significant part of the money that they had received to bring about the Revolution to the capitalists who had helped them in this respect. This and much besides points towards the very evident interest of certain occult brotherhoods of the West in the successful implementation in Eastern Europe, and especially in Russia, of the so-called "socialist experiment", which cost Russia and the other nations of the former USSR - according to the latest data - more than one hundred million human lives.

In his lectures, especially those that he gave during the First World War, Rudolf Steiner referred on several occasions to what the plans of these Western brotherhoods with regard to Russia amounted to.[11] According to him, their aim was (and it remains the same to this day) to oppose by every means available to them any development aimed at bringing about the sixth, Slavic cultural epoch, in order that the principle of the Spirit-Self might never descend to humanity. In this way the consciousness soul in its most materialistic form - as consistently spread throughout the world by the Western brotherhoods - would be conserved for ever. And in addition, their occult-political authority over humanity - towards which they have striven from the very beginning of their existence and which in our time is called "the new world order" - would unremittingly be maintained.

The method whereby these lodges of the West attain their principal purpose consists in the dissemination not merely of materialism but *super-materialism,* that is, materialism not as a new ideology but as something which totally permeates the whole of human life, including religion and occultism.[12] "They want to supermaterialise materialism itself, to establish in the world more materialism than has arisen as a result of the natural development of humanity in the fifth post-Atlantean epoch".[13] What this signifies in practice can be experienced today not only by Russia but by the whole of Europe, in the form of the cheapening of all spiritual values by the ubiquitous invasion of Americanism.

If, however, these Western brotherhoods were really to achieve their aims, the whole of earthly evolution would take an altogether different direction from what was originally intended by the good spiritual powers.

These dark intentions of the Western brotherhoods must be distinguished from the true spiritual and cultural tasks of the English-speaking peoples, which it is their responsibility to accomplish amongst mankind as the main representatives of the consciousness soul in the modern epoch.

On the other hand, in the secret brotherhoods referred to these peoples have what is perhaps the most dangerous enemy on the path of their true fulfilment. For this reason it is of particular importance for anthroposophists living in these countries to know about and understand their occult-political plans from a spiritual-scientific point of view.

The Third Level: Occult Streams of World History which lie at the Foundation of Bolshevism

In order to come closer to an understanding of the occult roots of Bolshevism, it is necessary to turn to the 7th century AD, or to be more precise to the time around the year 666. As is generally known, this number corresponds to the number of the beast from the abyss mentioned in the Apocalypse of St. John, the number of the Sun demon who is the principal adversary of Christ in our cosmos. Thus the first penetration of his forces into human history - a great thrust against earthly evolution as a whole - fell on that date. As a consequence of this demonic influence in the Near East, not far from modern Baghdad, there arose the so-called Academy of Gondhishapur. After the Emperor Justinian closed all Greek philosophical schools on the territory of the Byzantine Empire in the 6th century, most of the Greek philosophers and scholars were forced to seek refuge in Asia; and their wisdom had by the middle of the 7th century been gathered together in the aforesaid academy by a black initiate who was a human instrument of the Sun demon.[14]

With the help of this colossal pre-Christian wisdom gathered in the Academy of Gondhishapur, the Sun demon then intended to tempt humanity to enter prematurely into its consciousness-soul development, for which it was at the time utterly unready. In other words, that state of soul-life which was gradually to arise on Earth through man's own efforts only by the middle of the present, fifth cultural epoch, or the epoch of the consciousness soul (that is, by the middle of the third millennium), was - according to the plan of the Sun demon - to have suddenly overwhelmed humanity like a higher revelation already in the 7th century; and in souls unprepared for this it would have worked like a Satanic impulse of terrible destructive power. If this had happened in full measure, the whole of mankind would inevitably have entered upon a path of total demonisation.

The general situation in which European humanity then found itself can be characterised as follows. The greater part of the population of Europe was at that time still at the stage of development of the sentient soul. This was in the main a peasant population, able neither to read nor write, but for the most part already Christian. These were essentially simple people who, filled with ardent faith in the fundamental truths of Christianity, were guided by the Christian Church in a thoroughly authoritarian way - which was, however, appropriate, if one bears in mind mankind's stage of development at that time. Only very small numbers of educated people, amongst whom were not so much the nobility as the clergy and especially certain monastic orders, were bearers of the intellectual soul. As a rule, these people were grouped around monasteries, which were the principal centres of learning at that time, and communicated with one another in Latin. This impulse reached its culmination with the flowering of Scholasticism in the 13th century.

The Sun demon - whose occult name is Sorat - wanted to thrust his revelation of the consciousness soul into this structure of the European consciousness of that time, as a result of which all subsequent development amongst mankind of the impulse of the individual ego would have come to a halt. However, this plan of Sorat could not be fully implemented. It was prevented from an inner aspect by the forces issuing from the Mystery of Golgotha, and from an outer aspect by the appearance on the historical scene of Islam, which, like a hurricane sweeping away everything on its path, rapidly spread throughout the Near East. In this way the spike of the impulse of Gondhishapur was blunted.[15]

Nevertheless, the forces of Gondhishapur continued to work further in the Christian world even in this greatly weakened form. Thus under their direct influence the principle of the spirit was officially abolished in 869 AD at the Eighth "Ecumenical" Council in Constantinople for the entire Western Church* : whereas man's being had formerly consisted of a trichotomy of spirit, soul and body, henceforth - according to the dichotomy pronounced by the council - only the presence of body and soul was acknowledged, with the latter containing certain spiritual qualities.[16]   In this way the entire course of Western civilisation was given the materialistic direction which it continues to follow to this day.

The culmination of this process was the emergence in 19th century Europe of Darwin's theory of man's descent from animals and Marx's theory of the primacy of social existence over individual consciousness, which was in essence merely an extension of Darwinism to the realm of human social relationships.   Thus the abolition of the spirit in the 9th century served over ten centuries as a foundation for the abolition in Marxism also of the human soul.   In the minds of the majority of scientifically educated human beings, man is now conceived as a bodily form bereft of spirit and soul and regarded merely as a highly complex physical mechanism.

That science has no need to be inherently *materialistic* can be seen from what has arisen on the foundation of its methodology in Goetheanism and, above all, in modern spiritual science or Anthroposophy. However, it was the *materialistic* trend in science which led in the 19th century to Marxism and, in the 20th century, to its practical realisation in Bolshevism. Thus even purely historically it is possible to discern a direct line leading from the Academy of Gondhishapur in the 7th century to Bolshevism in the 20th century.

This finds further confirmation in the general spiritual-historical situation in Russia at the end of the 19th century and the beginning of the 20th.   At this time almost 80% of the population consisted of peasants, among whom around 75% were unable to read or write, that is, were altogether untouched by the principal fruits of Western civilisation. The general state of consciousness of this rural population was very similar to that which existed in Europe in the 7th century. As was the case then, the majority of Russian peasants retained a deep Christian faith, and in their

---

* The Eastern (Orthodox) Churche did not recognise the authority of this Eighth Council, and even today abides only by the first seven.

religious life they were guided by the Orthodox Church and its hierarchy. All this precisely corresponded to the essential character of the sentient soul, whose forces were still predominant in large sections of the population of Russia at the beginning of the 20th century. In addition, there existed in Russia a relatively small number of so-called cultured people, who were by and large bearers of intellectual-soul forces and, hence, had a particular fondness for Paris and France - that great metropolis of the intellectual soul. (This is why almost all the Russian intelligentsia rushed there as emigrés after the Bolsheviks had come to power.) Finally, Russia also had a very small segment of bearers of the consciousness soul, mainly those who were versed in the German idealistic philosophy of the early 19th century.

In this situation, the Bolsheviks tried forcibly to bring the consciousness-soul forces demonised by Sorat to the widest sections of the Russian people. Hence all the legislative measures of the Bolsheviks - such as collectivisation, industrialisation and especially the so-called "cultural revolution" - were really only serving one aim: imbuing as large a number of human souls as possible with the forces of Sorat.

As a result, the demonic impulse associated with the apocalyptic number of the beast - first unleashed to any significant degree upon European humanity in the 7th century - was from 1917 onwards made manifest in Russia in a far more successful way.

The Fourth Level: the Fall of the Spirits of Darkness

In his books and numerous lectures, Rudolf Steiner has on the foundation of spiritual-scientific research characterised the higher hierarchies working in the supersensible worlds, calling them by the names adopted in Christian tradition. Only if we take into account the power and sublimity of these beings of a higher stature than man will we be able to understand how easy it is for someone to regard an angel appearing to him in imagination as a revelation of God himself. Angels are, after all, no more than the nearest hierarchy to man. Above them stand higher beings - the Archangels or the guides of individual earthly peoples; and still higher are the Archai or the alternating leaders of entire historical epochs as experienced by the whole of humanity. These three categories of hierarchic spirits together form the Third Hierarchy, above which tower the spirits of the Second Hierarchy and - above them - the First Hierarchy, whose place lies immediately before the Holy Trinity which rules the world.

In his lectures Rudolf Steiner also describes the evolution of individual hierarchic spirits. He relates that the spirit who in Christian tradition bears the name of "Michael" has in the last third of the 19th century risen from the rank of Archangel to the higher rank of Archai or Time-Spirit, in order that he may over the course of the subsequent three or four centuries lead humanity as a whole. Rudolf Steiner specifies 1841 as the year when Michael began his ascent to the rank of the Archai.[17] From this moment he also began his battle with the Ahrimanic spirits of darkness who are active in the supersensible realm nearest to the Earth, that is, where Michael had to undertake his task as the new Time-Spirit. This battle with the spirits of darkness continued until 1879 and culminated in Michael's total victory. Now that he had freed this spiritual sphere from the Ahrimanic demons, he could embark upon the spiritual leadership of mankind. Thus the modern Michael epoch began.

However, this victory of Michael over the dragon had one highly important consequence for the rest of earthly evolution. For the place to which Michael in 1879 consigned the Ahrimanic spirits from the supersensible sphere nearest the Earth was the domain of human beings. Henceforth the dwelling-place of the demons became all the more often the human souls possessed by them.

The Book of Revelation refers to this event in the following words:

"Now war arose in heaven, Michael and his angels fighting against the dragon; and the dragon and his angels fought, but they were defeated and there was no longer any place for them in heaven. And the great dragon was thrown down, that ancient serpent, who is called the Devil and Satan, the deceiver of the whole world - he was thrown down to the Earth, and his angels were thrown down with him... Rejoice then, O heaven and you that dwell therein! But woe to you, O earth and sea, for the devil has come down to you in great wrath, because he knows that his time is short!" (ch. 12, vv. 7-9 and 12). *

According to Rudolf Steiner's spiritual-scientific research, this battle of Michael with the dragon had its particular time-structure: it began in 1841 and culminated with the victory of Michael in 1879, and then, after the passage of the same interval of time (38 years), in a certain sense it "returned to its starting-point".[18] This happened in 1917.

```
      1841                1879                1917
      L_____I_____I
```

---

* Of course, both this and other pictures in the Apocalypse relate not only to the context of the present by also to other spiritual events of both past and future.

This signifies that after Michael sent the Ahrimanic spirits of darkness down to the Earth, they had by 1917 reached their greatest power there - and this was reflected in the Bolshevik Revolution.

In the same period - from 1841 to 1917 - first Marxism arose and spread in Europe and then, as its practical realisation, Bolshevism. In 1848 Marx published his main programme-document, the Communist Manifesto, which began with the significant words: "A spectre is haunting Europe". This demonic "spectre" actually came to power in Russia in 1917.

We have now considered the four principal levels with which the greatest tragedy of Russia, not only of the 20th century but of its entire thousand-year history, was associated historically and metahistorically. These four levels when taken together reveal to us the full measure of the tragedy that took place and enable us to come closer to a real understanding of the terrible phenomenon of "Bolshevism".

Lenin and the Occult Foundations of Bolshevik Initiation

The Bolshevik Revolution in Russia was from the outset associated with the name of the founder of Bolshevism - Lenin. He was born in 1870 in the town of Simbirsk, in the Lower Volga region, that is, the region where the demonic beings whom, in the lecture "The Imagination of Europe", Rudolf Steiner characterises as the degenerate fauns and satyrs of ancient Greece had migrated on the etheric plane at the beginning of the Christian era. In the region between the Volga and the Urals these astral beings, by entering into a kind of supersensible marriage with one another, gave birth to frightening hybrids with a brilliant Luciferic intellectuality and with the power of an Ahrimanic will. Individuals such as Lenin and his associates were possessed by these demonic beings.[19]

When Lenin was 17 years old, he experienced the decisive event of his life. His older brother, who was a member of a terrorist organisation which had planned and attempted to commit the murder of the Russian tsar Alexander III, was arrested, sentenced to death and hanged. This event made an immense impression on his younger brother. For weeks he was in something of a dream-like state, until the great decision of his life matured within him: henceforth he knew for sure that he would be a revolutionary.

He began his subversive activity already while a student in the law department of Kazan University. After his first speeches as a student he was expelled from the university and was sent into exile for almost a year. In 1888 he returned from exile as a professional revolutionary who was possessed by a single idea: to overthrow tsarism and so avenge his brother's death. This principle of responding to every drop of blood with further streams of blood continued to be a feature of his political career. He succeeded in fully avenging his brother only in 1918, when on his orders the tsar and his entire family were savagely killed in Yekaterinburg.

The pseudo-science inaugurated by Lenin - subsequently called "Leninism" - had as its main task the artificial creation in the person of the Bolshevik of a "new man": the ancestor of a human race without precedent in history. If one tries to form an adequate picture of what this "new man" was to become, it is necessary to take into consideration Rudolf Steiner's assertion that in Bolshevism we have to do with a particular initiation with a terrible demonic power,[20] whose sources spring from the abyss, that is, from the sphere of activity of the beast of the Apocalypse. In the lecture-cycle on the Book of Revelation which he gave to the priests of the Christian Community, Rudolf Steiner directly indicated that the Sun demon, Sorat, was working through the Bolsheviks.[21] In this observation we have further confirmation of the connection which we have established between the Bolsheviks who seized power in Russia and the impulse of the Academy of Gondhishapur.

But what was the nature of Bolshevik initiation and in what did it consist? For all the Bolsheviks were without exception convinced materialists and atheists, and so their initiation could not have been based upon a *conscious* relationship with that demonic world from which it came. Nevertheless, their initiation was such that those who pursued it gradually became the obedient ego-less instruments of those demonic beings - "the dragon and his angels" - whom they served.

How this initiation came about in practice, and in what actual forms it manifested itself, could be observed with particular clarity by those who, like the author of these lines, spent their childhood and youth in Russia under the Bolshevik regime and were already anthroposophists.

The "Communist Party of the Soviet Union" was from the outset organised in accordance with a quite definite principle, which determined and strictly regulated all promotions in its members' service, that is, their promotion to higher posts in the hierarchical structure of the Party's nomenclature. In this principle one can see the signs of an infernal, utterly Ahrimanic initiation. The mechanism of this process was as follows. To begin with, a Party group of higher standing placed a definite task - consisting in the implementation of one or another programme - before another one of lower standing. In this programme were formulated the concrete goals of the Party at a given stage of the "communist project", which had to be accomplished by the Party group of lower standing, or a whole series of groups, "within a very strict time-frame". The general way in which the prescribed goal could be achieved was also defined in this programme. On the other hand, the actual paths and individual practical steps which were necessary in order to achieve it were not determined in the programme and were left to members of the group to consider. In order to find them these people needed a particular inspiration. And as all the aims and tasks which the Party set before them were always of an Ahrimanic nature, only a purely Ahrimanic inspiration could be allowed as a means of achieving the aim. Thus although the Bolsheviks knew nothing about Ahriman in their waking consciousness, without suspecting it they were constantly turning to him for help and advice - which they received, thereby beoming his consistent and faithful servants. For according to Rudolf Steiner, "these Party programmes correspond in the spiritual world to beings; and consequently, those who associate themselves with a Party programme become the followers of a particular being in the supersensible world".[22] In the course of their initiation, the Bolsheviks became the followers of such a mighty demonic being.

From this point of view, all the "ritual" assemblies of the Bolsheviks, and above all their Party gatherings and congresses on all levels, acquire a particular significance. Rudolf Steiner once expressed himself very radically about all such gatherings of materialists: "Why, for example, are these gatherings held? They are held in order to invoke the devil [Ahriman]! And this is so in a very direct sense, although people do not know this." These words were spoken four and a half years before the Bolsheviks seized power in Russia.[23]

But let us return to a consideration of the nature of their initiation. As has already been said, once a local Party group had received its particular assignment "from above" it would then have to find the speediest and most effective way of practically fulfilling it. For the successful implementation of a task, it was necessary for all participants to develop two inner qualities, without which the attainment of an Ahrimanic inspiration was impossible. One of these consisted in the development of a bare and abstract *intellectuality* bereft of feeling and devoid of conscience. This quality was consistently and comprehensively cultivated in all Bolshevik educational institutions, in Party schools, in numerous courses in Marxism-Leninism and so forth. The second quality was the cultivation in human beings of a criminal and, in all essentials, utterly animal *will*, which would not stop at anything where the achievement of its aims was concerned. These were the two main pillars on which Bolshevik initiation was founded. What they signified in practice was to be fully revealed in the so-called Stalinist epoch.

As they represented the complete opposite of true initiation, both these qualities in combination were capable of quickly and effectively destroying everything in the soul associated with feelings such as love, compassion, conscience and sacrificiality, which alone make a person a human individual in the full sense. In Bolshevik initiation all this was consistently replaced by a mechanistic working together of a cold, abstract intellectuality and a bestial will capable of any cruelty and crime for the sake of aims imposed - more often than not anonymously - from higher up in the Party hierarchy. This is the essential nature of the modern initiation of the beast, as a result of which the spirit of absolute evil, the spirit of Sorat, turns man into its obedient instrument by killing, and taking the place of, the human soul.

Once the group concerned had carried out the task placed before it, a Party inspection immediately followed, which had the object of establishing who of all the participants in the implementation of the programme had shown his worth most "consciously" and actively and, hence, had contributed the most to its ultimate success. Such a Party worker proved by his actions that the underlying motive of his thoughts and deeds was the endeavour to further the implementation of the "decree" of the Party with all his strength and with all the means at his disposal. From an occult point of view he was thereby demonstrating a highly developed capacity for the receiving of Ahrimanic inspirations, and could therefore be elevated in rank, that is, promoted to the next level of the Party nomenclature. Then the whole process was again repeated, though on a higher plane. A new "assignment" - the fulfilment of which demanded from those engaged in it even more radical actions and an even more cunning intellect - again descended "from above", though from a more influential Party group. After this the process described above of "occult selection" was repeated again and again until the "Politburo" was reached. In this way the "new man", the repesentative of the "radiant" communist future, was systematically bred in the womb of the Party. The most effective means of training for this path that has been described was a boundless *fear*, by which all those participating in this Ahrimanic initiation were continually gripped. And this fear was not without foundation. For anyone who, in this artificial process of selection based upon identifying with the most radical powers of evil, came up against the limits of his ability to receive Ahrimanic inspirations, immediately became superfluous to the Party and was therefore pronounced an "enemy of the people" and stripped of all his offices, after which his physical annihilation generally followed. This is why waves of bloody purges regularly swept through all levels of the Party hierarchy. And the endless show-trials of "enemies of the people" served as a means of frightening the rest, thus significantly hastening the process of Ahrimanic initiation.

This combination of a cunning intellect with an animal-like will led in a short time to the total atrophy in the human beings concerned of the middle or heart realm, the main source of their moral impulses. At the same time this led to the over-development of lower instincts which could no longer be restrained, both in the intellectual and in the will sphere. Such soul-forces as wonder, compassion and conscience, with which is connected the growth in a human being of his individual sense of morality and personal resonsibility for what is happening in the world, were to be completely destroyed in the "new man". This meant the literal annihilation of what gave him the right to call himself a human being - his individual ego, which, as the bearer of his spirit, has the task of guiding all the powers of his soul. Rudolf Steiner called this spirit-imbued, autonomous rulership over the soul-forces in thinking, feeling and will on the part of the individual ego the life in the consciousness soul, and he regarded the unfolding of its forces within man as the principal task of the modern fifth post-Atlantean cultural epoch. Whereas the Bolshevik initiation led to the total destruction of the consciousness soul, as a result of which the human ego was no longer able to lead an existence worthy of a human being and inevitably descended into a demonic, sub-human realm.

In the Gospel of St. Matthew this condition is characterised by the words of the prophet Daniel about "the abomination of desolation standing in the holy place" (ch. 24 v. 15). What is meant here is the entry of demons into the holy of holies of man's being, where by rights only the forces of the ego can work. And if they are driven out, a human being is turned into no more than an animal with a cunning mind, that is, he becomes a being who in his subconscious is actually possessed by the demons of Sorat. This is the main fruit of Bolshevik initiation.

The Metamorphosis of Conscience and the Appearance of the Etheric Christ

The Academy of Gondhishapur tried prematurely to imbue humanity with the forces of the consciousness soul, in order wholly to paralyse the development that was intended for it in our fifth cultural epoch. In 20th century Russia, Bolshevik initiation, in which a demonised consciousness soul was to be put at the service of powers of apocalyptic evil, was used for the attainment of the same aim. The human ego could not live and work in a soul that was so imbued with powers of evil. As a result, anyone who passed through Bolshevik initiation had ultimately to be deprived of his ego, that is, deprived of what alone makes him man on Earth. It was this loss of the ego by those who had gone through Bolshevik initiation which led to those enormities inconceivable to ordinary human consciousness, crimes which from the outset accompanied the entire history of the Bolsheviks' tenure of power, both in Russia and, subsequently, in the other countries dependent upon it. For the absence in a human being of his ego opens the gates for the demons of Sorat to enter his soul.

The image in the Book of Revelation of the locusts with human faces and lions' teeth (ch. 9) refers to these human beings who have been deprived of their ego.[24]   Moreover, it relates not only to the leaders of the Bolshevik or National Socialist movements but also to many future events. For in the 20th century mankind has indeed entered the apocalyptic period of its history.

The modern appearance of Christ in an etheric form on Earth marked the beginning of the Little Apocalypse or the radical *separation of souls* into those consciously choosing the path of the good and those consciously choosing the path of evil; that is, those embarking upon the path of Christian or anti-Christian *initiation*, a path which either leads or does not lead to a meeting with the Etheric Christ in the spiritual world nearest to the earthly sphere.

At the Council of Constantinople the demons of Sorat succeeded in so darkening the consciousness of the leaders of the Christian Church at that time that under their influence the principle of the spirit was excluded from the conception of man. By this means, highly favourable conditions were created in Western civilisation for the subsequent influence of evil powers, especially those which today more than anything else place obstacles in the path of a true understanding of the nature of the human ego and its central significance for the present and future evolution of mankind. One can say: if in the 9th century the Church Fathers had not abolished the spirit, Bolshevism would have been impossible in the 20th century. For it arose out of the abolition of the soul which followed the abolition of the spirit, with the result that man was brought down to the level of a thinking animal bereft of an ego.

The human ego has a primordial connection with the spiritual world. Thus wherever a human being consciously overcomes his egotism and acts out of his own moral intuitions, which have the ego as their source, the voice of conscience gives its assent to such actions; and in the voice of conscience people today are all the more often able to discern the Etheric Christ speaking to them. The experience of the Etheric Christ working through conscience is in our time the only power able to overcome those forces of evil in the soul which in the 20th century called the phenomenon of Bolshevism into existence and which - if bounds are not placed upon it - will continue to work on amongst mankind in the future, thus putting its very existence in question.

However, this experience of Christ is no more than the beginning of His modern revelation to mankind. For through the further development of conscience, which will come about under the influence of Christ, the faculty of an imaginative beholding of a person's own karma will arise within him, that is, of those deeds which he must accomplish in future in order to balance it out.[25] Such a radical metamorphosis of the forces of conscience in earthly evolution will be associated with Christ's becoming the Lord of the karma of the whole of mankind from the end of the 20th century.[26]

The Russian people, who are in our time called to become the living *conscience of mankind*, have a very important mission which is associated with this task of totally transforming the forces of conscience. But this potential of the Russian people will be fulfilled only when, with the help of spiritual science, Russians seek truly to know the spiritual beings who oppose this in earthly evolution and consciously withstand them in their souls through the power of the Etheric Christ, who is now mankind's principal helper in its battle with the powers of evil in the apocalyptic epoch that has now begun.

"In the world you have tribulation;
But be of good cheer:
I have overcome the world."

(John 16:33)

References

[1] See Rudolf Steiner, GA 173 and 174 (*The Karma of Untruthfulness* vols. 1 and 2) and GA 186 (some lectures translated as *The Challenge of the Times*; *Social and Anti-Social Forces in Man*).

[2] See Ludwig Polzer-Hoditz, *Das Testament Peters des Grossen und der Kampf gegen den Geist*, Dornach 1989.

[3] See further in Niall Ferguson, *The Pity of War*, Harmondsworth 1998.

[4] A photograph of this picture was published in the book, *Helmuth von Moltke, 1848-1916. Dokumente zu sienem Leben und Wirken*. vol. 1, Basel 1993 (English translation entitled *Light for the New Millennium*, London 1997).

[5] This Pan-Slavic movement of the end of the 19th century should not be confused with the strivings of the Slavophils in the middle of the same century. the Slavophils never pursued political aims.

[6] Rasputin was killed as a result of a second attempt on his life on 30th December 1916.

[7] Excerpts from this letter were published in a book by V. Fedyushin: *Russlands Sehnsucht nach Spiritualitat. Theosphie, Anthroposophie und die Russen*, Schaffhausen 1988.

[8] See note 1.

[9] See note 1. This map has since been published in a number of anthroposophical books and articles, most recently in Terry Boardman's book *Mapping the Millennium. Behind the Plans of the New World Order*, London 1998.

[10] See, for example, Anthony C. Sutton's book, *Wall Street and the Bolshevik Revolution*, Western Australia 1981.

[11] See note 1 and Rudolf Steiner, *Gegenwärtiges und Vergangenes im Menschengeiste* (GA167, not translated).

[12] The teachings of Alice Bailey represent the clearest example of such an occult materialism. See S. O. Prokofieff, *The East in the Light of the West Part II: The Teachings of Alice Bailey in the light of Christian Esotericism* (not published in English; German tr. Dornach 1997).

[13] Rudolf Steiner, *The Karma of Untruthfulness vol. 2* (GA 174), lecture of 20th January 1917.

[14] Rudolf Steiner, GA 184, lecture of 12th October 1918 (*Three Streams in the Evolution of Mankind*).

[15] Ibid

[16] See ibid., the lecture of 11th October 1918. Regarding the Eighth Council in Constantinople, see the collection of articles entitled *Der Kampf um das Menschenbild. Das achte Ökumenische Konzil von 869 und seine Folgen*, ed. H. H. Schoffler, Dornach 1986.

[17] Rudolf Steiner, *The Fall of the Spirits of Darkness* (GA 177), lecture of 14th October 1917, and also GA 174a, lecture of 17th February 1918 (*The Mission of the Archangel Michael*).

[18] Ibid., lecture of 17th February 1918.

[19] See above

[20] Rudolf Steiner, *Polarities in the Evolution of Mankind* (GA 197), lecture of 13th June 1920.

[21] Rudolf Steiner, *The Book of Revelation and the Work of the Priest* (GA 346) lecture of 12th September 1924.

[22] Rudolf Steiner, *Spritual Science as a Foundation for Social Forms* (GA 199), lecture of 7th August 1920.

[23] Rudolf Steiner, *The Effects of Spiritual Development* (GA 145), lecture of 28th March 1913.

[24] See Rudolf Steiner, *The Book of Revelation and the Work of the Priest* (GA 346).

[25] Rudolf Steiner, *The Christ Impulse and the Deveopment of Ego-Consciousness* (GA 116), lecture of 8th May 1910.

[26] Rudolf Steiner, *From Jesus to Christ* (GA 131), lecture of 14th October 1911.

Computers and Intelligence

Harlan Gilbert

I. Introduction

We are faced today with startling examples of computers emulating what we think of as intelligent behaviour. Not only do they control our factories' machines, perform secretarial tasks and keep track of our businesses' books, but they also seem to respond - sometimes even quite reasonably - to enquiries, play chess and predict our weather. In the face of such convincing achievements we readily assume that there must be *some* form of intelligence present and active in the computer.

Because we can see the workings of such simple mechanisms as mousetraps or mills we are not normally deceived into thinking that these are anything but purely mechanical devices. As technology becomes more sophisticated, however, we can no longer observe its workings, nor as non-specialists can we readily comprehend the principles by which the mechanisms operate. When this happens we may easily lose sight of their character as machines. This is particularly true of highly complex electronic devices, of computers. We may even begin to believe that they show signs of intelligence simply because *our* intelligence can no longer follow the workings of the technology that produces the results we see. That is to say, because they are not *simple mechanisms*, their nature *simply as mechanism* becomes more difficult to discern.

Let us take an analogy. We know that mousetraps can react to the presence of mice. We attribute neither a hunting instinct, a pleasure in the kill nor an intelligent plan to the mousetrap, for it is obvious that its working is purely mechanical. Because mousetraps are quite simple mechanisms, it is readily apparent that they are endowed with neither intelligence nor a feeling life. This case is a useful reminder that actions or reactions, however analogous to those of organisms imbued with an inner life these may appear, in no way prove the existence of instincts, feelings or intelligence.

Computers show a range of actions and reactions that often lead us to use the term 'artificial intelligence'. It is a short step from here to go on to ascribe an actual intelligence to them. What is the difference between actual and 'artificial' intelligence?

II. The Simulation of Intelligence

To understand the actual nature of the phenomenon often referred to as 'artificial intelligence' we must look back to the origins of computing devices. An early theorist of these devices laid down principles to which all modern computers essentially still adhere. He described the archetypal computer as consisting of a series of digital states (which can be imagined as a perhaps very long row of lights, each of which are either on or off at any moment) and a linear 'tape' of information. This 'information tape' simply consists of a series of positions, each of which is either punched or not punched (marked or not marked). With each position that the computer encounters on the tape, the computer's state (lights) may change, but only according to certain pre-determined and fixed rules. The limitation laid down is that the new state of the computer after this encounter (its new pattern of lights) must be *completely* determined by the operation of these fixed rules upon the computer's current state and the tape position currently encountered. After each of these occurrences, the tape may also be moved forward or backward one position; this too must be dependent upon fixed and pre-determined rules.

It is easy to show that - despite some apparent superficial divergences[1] - the modern computer still essentially conforms to these original principles. That is to say, *every* digital computer operates according to (and only according to) the sequence of mechanical[2] operations described above. Thus there can be no question of attributing any more *actual* intelligence

[1] For example, computers now normally process a (fixed) number of positions, or bits, simultaneously and often have more than one source of information. The reception of data in either of these ways can also be achieved by the device posited by the original model, though more slowly and cumbersomely. Even the occasional use of so-called 'random generators' - devices which create more or less unpredictable (random) streams of data can be shown to be no exception to the original model.

[2] The term mechanical might be questioned given the electronic nature of the devices. All digital computers depend on two-state (on or off) switches. Whether these are effected by mechanical switching apparatus, vacuum tubes, transistors, printed circuits or light arrays affects the size, speed and energy consumption involved, but not the essential principle. All these devices simply simulate mechanical (two-state) switches, losing the character of their actual technical workings and material nature thereby. The logic employed is actually derived from mechanical, not electrical --principles. In other words, the computer's mechanistic logic is in question here and not the technology used to implement this.

to these highly complex but still essentially mechanical reactions than could be attributed to a mechanical loom or typewriter. What, then, do we mean by artificial intelligence?

Intelligence presupposes the ability to conceive the world in various ways. Aristotle categorized four fundamental aspects of the world: everything can be seen to have an original cause, a purpose in the grand world plan, a form and finally a substance or material of composition.[3]

The intelligence of a human being consists not least in the capacity for a fluid (thus playful[4]) relationship to these four ways of conceiving the world. Human intelligence normally understands *or can come to understand* each of these modes of understandings' contributions to the current situation and can adjust its relationship to them both sensibly and creatively, that is, 'intelligently'. Even a cat on the hunt for a mouse will react to many unexpected events appropriately. It will change its intention if appropriate (e.g., a dog appears or the mouse doesn't show). It will modify its approach (technique) if necessary (e.g., its hiding place is seen or the mice change their strategies). It will adapt its conception of form and of substance (e.g., it will eventually learn to ignore a child trying to fool it with an imitation mouse on a string, and when a bird flies by or a bowl of milk is brought it will happily seek out an alternative source of its breakfast).

Simulated ('artificial') intelligence can only adequately react to any situations foreseen by the developers: 'If the yarn runs out, stop the machine'. We do not consider the *loom* clever for stopping when there is no more yarn: rather its inventor and makers. There are, indeed, so-called 'learning programmes' for computers[5] through which they react increasingly appropriately through experience (e.g., handwriting recognition programmes that improve their accuracy each time they are corrected). These are not exceptions to this principle of mechanical reaction any more than a mechanical device for adjusting the loom tension on the basis of the already produced weave would be. *The possibilities for recognizing and adjusting are actually static,* and *truly* unpredicted[6] events (e.g., a person writing Chinese, or backwards, or employing an unfamiliar letter - á, ö, ø -

---

[3] Aristotle also formulated the principles of logic which underlie - two thousand years later - the workings of modern computing devices. Aristotle's historical connexion with the principles and evolution of computing will be shown to be deep and essential.

[4] Playful, in Schiller's sense of the word, that is, the ability to explore and move freely between polarities.

[5] I mean here programmes whereby the computer is meant to learn, not those intended to teach the user.

[6] Not necessarily unpredictable, but unpredicted! How often do we wish that the programmers had predicted the 'obvious' potential for a given situation which has in fact arisen.

or putting the wrong document into the machine, or the right one upside down) will always show up the precise limits of the makers' forethought. Note well: *we encounter the makers' intelligence (and the limits of their forethought), not the intelligence or forethought of the machine; the latter has neither of these.*

A human being in any of these situations would discover the nature of the problem and try to find a way to sort it out; a computer can, at best (that is, if it even discovers that there is an unexpected 'input') give some form of response equivalent to: 'Unpredicted situation encountered. The limit of the technology has been surpassed. Please call an intelligent being.' In other words, a human being can learn to read Chinese or ask for a translation, can learn the pronunciation of an unfamiliar letter and to check if the document is correct and face up. A computer can only be re-programmed to do these things.

In addition, a computer cannot be said to approach any sort of conception of any of our ways of experiencing the world: cause, purpose, form *or* substance. All that it has is *data* - electronic states, really - which *we* then choose to interpret as being 'about' the world.

The extraordinary range of simulated intelligence already and soon to be achieved must not and indeed cannot fool us. Computers are unintelligent machines, and anyone who works with such devices quickly discovers that the user's behaviour must be made equally unintelligent, that is, that we must conform precisely to the machine's severely limited schema. Any behaviour of ours that is outside this schema is either ignored or promptly leads to unexpected and normally undesirable results. The computer is of course completely unable to become aware that it is trapped in such a schema. It is left to the human being to discover this, and to progressively discover the nature, possibilities and limits of the machine's schema (this schema is often known as its programming).

Sophisticated machines remain machines, whatever the level of sophistication reached. There are computer scientists who await a breakthrough of 'quality' through increasing 'quantity' of sophistication, but though a crystal appears vastly different to a stone, it will never become a plant. The degree of complexity of organization does not change an organism's nature or level on the hierarchy of realms of being. A machine cannot be other than a machine through being very intricate in its workings.

When a radio plays music, a child will wonder where the singer is. She will assume that there is in fact a musician inside the box. We as sophisticated adults will of course smile at the question, for we know that there is no singer in the little black box but only a mere reproduction of music. We, however, must be careful not to do something similar when faced with sophisticated modern computing devices.

We must learn to look at computers and know that there is no intelligence there, but simply a cleverly made recording of intelligence, subject to all the limitations and distortions of any recording, and above all to those of its fashioners.

Part III A. The Nature of Intelligence

There was a time when meadow, grove and stream,
The earth and every common sight
To me did seem
Apparell'd in celestial light,
The glory and the freshness of a dream.
It is not now as it has been of yore;-
Turn wheresoe'er I may,
By night or day,
The things which I have seen I now can see no more!

W. Wordsworth

How is it possible that even a remotely plausible or momentarily convincing illusion or simulation of intelligence can be produced by a mere array of switching devices?[7] What do we mean by intelligence, if this looks like a case of it? Which aspects of intelligence are in fact present in the machine's behaviour and which are absent? Finally, what is the ultimate limit of the simulation? How far can it be taken?

Human intelligence has actually been on a path of transformation, in some senses decline, for a very long time now. Wordsworth describes how even our very perception has changed in this process: 'The things which I have seen I now can see no more!' When human intelligence first awoke long ago, it was indeed in the form of a direct perception of the Being and Beings implicit in and indwelling all things. This was the Paradise situation: man lived face to face with God.

This underwent a transformation as man took hold of and incarnated

---

[7] It seems worth emphasizing again that this question is not different in kind from wondering how it is possible that a fairly convincing simulation of music can come from a (slightly different) box of gadgetry; our experience of music and our experience of intelligence must be open to being fooled by replications or imitations of both. It is worth exploring the reasons for this.

into successively deeper layers of his own being. Man began to experience his soul life and thereby gained a first awareness of himself as a being having an existence separate from the rest of the cosmos. He gained the experience of being an individual, however, at the cost of losing his direct experience of the rest of the world - and indeed of himself - as *individuality*, as being. Previously he had dwelt amidst a world populated with beings and knew not that he was one as well. Now, he 'knew himself' to be separate but had lost the direct awareness of all other beings. The world of being, of direct communication with and experience of the Gods, was lost (the Fall from Paradise). A door was closed. Only the *revelations* of these beings were now experienced, while a veil hid the beings themselves, though their presence or existence could still be sensed dimly behind the veil.

This was the temptation offered: *be yourself as a God*; unsaid was, *but lose God*, be lost to God.

Man now experienced the separateness that gives the possibility of knowing and choosing between good and evil. He thus gained the experience of an independent soul life. But this soul life was only capable of experiencing the world at a *soul* level, no longer at that of pure spirit. The highest sense had been lost, that for the ego of another being. Indeed, man now experienced even his own individuality only through this soul experience, not as ego per se, not through his spirit. More precisely: he no longer had a direct experience of himself as *individuality*, only as *individual*. A veil had also fallen between his *own* higher being and his consciousness.

It was at this time that initiation acquired its first task: to reawaken the experience of *Being* in man. 'For now we see through a glass, darkly: but then face to face: now I know in part; but then shall I know even as also I am known.'[8]

Intelligence was now devoted to comprehending the revelations of the 'Gods', of the world's beings. This included as a matter of course the beings of the natural world as well as fellow human beings and being of the higher worlds. Every daisy and buttercup spoke to man's soul at this time: the world was one of revelation everywhere.

But this experience also had to be lost to man. As mankind incarnated more deeply, the experience of the body's own life forces and organic activity was entered into. Through this, the ability to experience the world as revelation was lost. Now, instead of world revelation the *activity* of the world was present before us. Before, everything had been experienced as speaking a word of the great cosmic language. Now our ability to perceive the cosmic words was lost, but in exchange man himself gained the ability

[8] I Corinthians 13, 12.

to speak. Before, all things had spoken to him, and he was present in the world and had heard their revelation. He himself had only spoken as they did, as cosmic revelation poured through him. Now man could speak out of himself - and this was new - but his speech was not revelation, not even of revelation of man's own being. It was purely subjective *speaking*, speech as subjective activity. Speech had fallen, and the direct sense perception of the world as Word was lost.

Intelligence was now only active as a capacity to comprehend the world of driving impulses and effects (modern popular astrology's descriptions of the constellations and planets retain an impression from these experiences).

Mankind went further yet. Man began to experience himself as a purely physical being. In Renaissance times this began, curiously enough, as an experience of rejuvenation, in a reflection, as it were, of the balanced Greek experience of the life forces in nature and the life forces in the human organism. Now, however, the life forces were no longer experienced, but rather the physical body itself. The decline made itself felt rapidly; the world of inter-connected activity was lost and only the dead, silent, outer sense-impressions were to be found. For the first time, man experienced himself as being fully disconnected from the rest of the world. The cosmos was no longer experienced as working in and through him; he himself was now responsible for his own physical existence, and felt himself to be alone in this task.

Intelligence now was given the task of grasping physical existence, of making it possible to comprehend and take hold of the outer physical world. Modern natural science, the science of the material nature and physical workings of the world, was born.

Man had previously experienced the activity and influences of the world working through him; now, for the first time, he experienced himself as being independently active. But his activity was that of the physical body, not of the life forces. What we experience now as activity is our physical activity and the physical activity around us; the real activity of the life forces has been lost to our consciousness.

Such has been the situation for the last half-millennium.[9]

B. Intelligence applied to the Physical World

Through the development over approximately the last five centuries of an increasing consciousness of his physical body it has become possible for man

---

[9] The author would like to express his debt to Rudolf Steiner's descriptions of human and world evolution, in particular his *Leading Thoughts*, without which this chapter could not have been written in this form.

to create machines which imitate various bodily functions externally. The physical experience of the limbs as mechanical apparatus has led to the development of a wide variety of machinery that works on analogous mechanical principles: for example, digging, hammering, sawing, kneading, weaving and sewing machines. These 'limb-machines', which generally deal with solid matter, have been driven by devices that use the rhythmic circulation of fluids[10] primarily to transform energy into usable power: water wheels, steam and diesel engines, the modern automobile engine, turbines.[11] Finally, we come to the (usually electronic) devices which record and process information as well as controlling machines of the first two types.

We have systematized a great deal of our thinking over the last few centuries. The process actually began with Aristotle, who formulated the rules of logic in the fourth century BC. He thereby gave thinking a direction towards understanding the material world and its laws and away from the imaginative, pictorial thinking that had previously held sway. This Aristotelian logic was practised for two thousand years and has been absorbed into humanity's evolution (who is unfamiliar with causal logic today?). It has accompanied and perhaps even guided the process of incarnation into our physical brains and thereby allowed us to use their workings as a (perhaps largely unconscious) model for the computing devices of the last century.

We are now all masters of many intellectual faculties which were reserved for a rare few not many centuries ago. Reading, writing, calculating and logical analysis were rare accomplishments until the Renaissance and the popular revolutions of the eighteenth century brought their impulses towards universal intellectual education. We usually speak of universal education[12] without noting that the education of many skills - spinning, weaving, milking, mowing and reaping, etc. - *was* nearly universal in earlier days and has been nearly completely replaced by the intellectual skills taught in our schools today.

It is these intellectual achievements that are capable of being mechanized by computer.

---

[10] Or the flow of air: windmills, etc.

[11] There is a functional relationship between the flow of blood through the chambers of the heart to that of the flow of fuel through the cylinders of an engine: the valves and cylinders of the latter have an analogous working to the valves and chambers of the former. Of course, the heart serves more as a regulator of rhythm for a circulation which originates outside of itself, whereas the engine's driving power is located inside of the engine itself; the latter could be said to be an inversion of the former.

[12] It should be noted that the Renaissance brought an impulse towards an education much less universal but also much less one-sidedly intellectual than the later movement for popular education. The value set in Renaissance times on artistic capacity and sensitivity and on practical skills gave expression to a humanism to which the later Rationalists had little access.

In order to simulate an intellectual skill on a computer, this skill must be reduced to a series of mechanically executable steps. In particular, these steps must be capable of being translated into a series of automatic operations on a range of electronically simulated noughts and ones ('off's and 'on's).[13] It is this reduction of intellectual work to a series of primitive operations on a series of binary values which results in the highly impressive achievements of calculation, presentation and systematized record keeping with which we are familiar. The history of computing is thus in part the history of the reduction of intelligent activity to mechanical process. Important to note here is that this mechanization of thinking has often *preceded* computerization. Bookkeeping, for example, became a rather dull, mechanical activity long before computers took on the task. The task has often become *fit* for computers (and unfit for human beings) long before it has been given over to the machines. To a considerable extent, human beings are being freed from dreary repetitive *intellectual* tasks through the activity of computers just as we are being freed from wearying, backbreakingly repetitive *mechanical* tasks by the busy practical machinery which surrounds us.

Perhaps it is worth emphasizing one last time, however, that though a great deal of creative ability and intelligence are devoted to developing the machines in our times, these same human creative abilities and active, penetrative understanding can never be accessible to automatic machinery. The latter can only take over processes devoid of these qualities.

The physical processes of the metabolic-limb, rhythmic and sense-nervous systems in man are accompanied by *soul* processes. His limb activity is directed by an active *will*, his rhythmic activity of the circulation of fluids and of air is interwoven by a life of *feeling*, his nervous system is active as the expression of meaningful *thought activity*. In the machine, none of these soul qualities is present; it is as if we had before us a being that is just limb movement, without direction, or one that is purely endless rhythmic circulation, without significance, or one that is purely calculation, without understanding. Of course, man can employ these dumb servants for his own purposes, significance and understanding. Who is it that we are employing here, though? Perhaps at times we will even begin to ask: who is serving whom?

---

[13] Modern computers provide the possibility of using pre-established groupings of these primitive operations so that the human being need not always break everything down into the extremely simple steps that the computer is actually capable of performing. This work is accomplished by programming languages and user interfaces. This 'user-friendly' (and programmer-friendly) visible face of the computer conceals further the actual operations of the devices. This concealment, of course, has concomitant advantages as well as disadvantages.

IV. The Role of "Artificial Intelligence" in Earth's Evolution

Mankind is becoming increasingly responsible for guiding the evolution of the earth. The mineral world of earth and stone is already increasingly being given form by man's activity, while the plant and animal realms are to a substantial extent subject to our influence or even control and are becoming increasingly dependent upon our direction for their evolution. This is a valid and extremely important part of our task on earth: we are (becoming) the lords of all creation. The difficulty here is to keep the balance between two extremes. One extreme is the wish to deny this task and give nature over to 'itself' (a self that it has not yet developed). The other is the contrary tendency to impose our might and will on the lower realms of creation without perceiving and having respect for their own nature and character. The balance between these could be described as the human being's attempt to exercise a respectful yet active guidance over the realms of nature.

Nature was once under the wise guidance of spiritual forces; long ago this included being cultivated by man. Nature has never been truly 'left to itself'; it has always been part of a larger whole. The Gods have now withdrawn from their creation and have drawn back from their active guidance of mankind as well. We are thus confronted with a new situation, and one for which we shall increasingly have to take responsibility.

A responsible attitude towards nature implies an ever-increasing consciousness of the natural world's diversity, rhythms and inter-dependencies: its ecology. Unless we respect, preserve and enhance these, treating them as if these beings were our own children, we shall lose the right and the capacity to live in a natural world. Indeed, our *own* health and balance depend upon our maintaining a caring relationship towards the beings of nature.

We must remain modest about our present capacities to be true cultivators of the earth. Thousands of years - indeed, epochs and aeons - of work and research lie ahead before we shall again be able to do justice to this task. To understand the full magnitude of the task we must look back to how spiritual beings once played a role in establishing the original physical basis for our own being to enter into evolution on the physical plane.

Mankind evolved under the guidance of higher beings.[14] Already during the earliest, so-called Saturn phase of earth's evolution certain of these

---

[14] Here again I must express my debt to Rudolf Steiner; without his research into the earth's evolution (see his Occult Science: An Outline) this chapter could not have been written at all. The considerations here however have been extended to computers and man's role as a co-creator responsible for the realms of nature; the responsibility for these is wholly my own.

had the task to lay down the archetype of man's physical body. These first forms of physical bodies were *only* physical, that is, empty of life, consciousness or self-awareness. Shaped from the Earth's still incoherent warmth-substance (analogous to the masses of rock underlying the earth of today, though made up of warmth rather than mineral substance), a two-fold structure was developed. One part of the structure was formed of warmth-substance with a more static tendency while the other portion was formed of a more active substance, a less physically substantial warmth more inclined to interchange with the environment. Thus there was a more physical warmth in the interior structure and a more enlivened (etheric) warmth in the exterior structure. These were early stages of our skeleton and sense organs, respectively.

The beings which particularly impressed their character upon the physical bodies of this first phase of mankind's (and earth's) evolution had the cosmic task and gift of becoming Spirits of Personality. In shaping portions of the world's primeval warmth-substance into new forms, a task to which many kinds of beings contributed, they had the particular task of giving expression to their characteristic element of personality. In Rudolf Steiner's words, 'these Beings communicate to the particles of the Saturn body a semblance of the character of personality. Yet personality itself is not yet present in the warmth element on Saturn, but only its mirrored image - as it were, an outer shell or husk of personality.'[15] The Spirits of Personality experienced the *reflection* of the personality which they had developed streaming back to them from what they had shaped.[16] They had imprinted the warmth bodies with the outer form of a being equipped with personality, but no actual personality was present in these bodies. The beings thus had no inner life, but gave the appearance of having one through their form.

Our responsibility and capacity for the evolution of new beings is analogous to what was once done for us. In the diffuse sphere of warmth available as a medium at the moment when the basis for our own physical bodies was laid down, beings of evolution three stages ahead of man established forms which would serve as the basis for man's physical body to evolve.[17] Now, three stages of world-evolution later, having evolved life forces, consciousness and self-consciousness, man is coming to the time of

[14] Rudolf Steiner, *Occult Science*, Rudolf Steiner Press, 1963, p.116.

[16] 'Throughout the whole of Saturn there is no inwardness; but the Spirits of Personality behold and recognize the image of their own inwardness, in that it streams out to them as warmth from Saturn.' Steiner, p.121.

[17] Following Steiner: Man-Angel-Archangel-Archai (Spirits of Personality); thus three stages separate man and the Archai or Spirits of Personality.

his own responsibility for the evolution of other beings, and indeed for
helping to form physical bodies from which new evolutions may develop.
In his work with the mineral realm, three kingdoms below his own level of
evolution,[18] man has an analogous task to that of the Archai at the time
when these helped form the basis for man's physical body. The mineral
world is now in the position in which man was to be found during the
Saturn phase of earth's evolution. Man now has the task of taking the
material substance of the earth and giving it new forms. Into these new
forms beings awaiting the chance to enter into evolution can incarnate.

There are various directions which this can take. We can picture for
instance the awesome transformation involved in reshaping masses of
incoherent rock into the magnificence of Chartres Cathedral. According to
Steiner, a work such as Chartres will arise in metamorphosed form during
the phase of Earth's evolution which will follow our own. Such artistic
creations will appear again as flowers appear during our phase of
evolution, that is, equipped with life forces and capable of growth and
decay, though with a mineral body. New life forces capable of enlivening
a body of stone will permeate their transformed existence. We must
visualize here magnificent flower-like organisms with crystalline
blossoms, a more stone-like leaf and stem region and then truly stony
roots[19], and then imagine such a transformation of Chartres Cathedral or
the Parthenon, Hagia Sophia and Goetheanum (to name but a few
examples).

Now, other physical structures which man has created will also
provide paths of incarnation for beings. In particular, let us turn to the
devices known as computers. Computers are fashioned by shaping mineral
substance - crystals (traditionally silicon) and conductive metals - into
incredibly complex and finely fashioned patterns of electronic circuitry.
These transformations of the mineral realm are an expression of something
fundamentally different from the exquisite artistry of the above-mentioned
works of architecture. Architectural works are always a combination of the
practical will, aesthetic feeling and the insightful mind (Vitruvius[20] called
these 'structure, beauty and function'). The design of computer circuits is
not so influenced by aesthetic considerations and the functions aimed at no

---

[18] That is, Man-Animal Kingdom-Plant Kingdom-Mineral Kingdom.

[19] It should be emphasized that the terms, 'flower', 'blossom', 'leaf' and 'root' can only be used
by analogy. The forms of beings on Jupiter (the next phase of earth's evolution) will be
radically different from present-day forms.

[20] Vitruvius: a Roman architect who - in the earliest known treatise on architecture - set down
these three as fundamental architectural principles.

longer include the full range of human life.[21] Computer circuitry is purely determined by the rational intellect's logic working at a refinement and complexity, but also at a merciless absoluteness of principle previously unknown in world evolution. An automobile engine, otherwise a triumph of modern precision engineering, is but a child's toy in comparison.

What beings will find a path to incarnation through these formations (both now and in future planetary phases)? We saw that the wondrously complex harmony of Chartres can be imagined transformed in a future evolutionary phase into a flower having all the lovely, wonderfully complex harmony of the cathedral yet equipped with life - a mineral form capable of growth and decay. When we come to the integrated chip, the computer, we must imagine a living, growing being with the laws of *these* devices as their basis: one-sided, virtually a parasitic virus of the future earth. Incapable of existence except by feeding on beings of more well-rounded capacity to live and evolve, these could only have one purpose: to reproduce themselves and extend their crystalline maze of logic over all the earth.

The universe we now live in was formed out of *wisdom*. The microcosmic correspondence to this cosmic wisdom is our human intelligence, which has evolved through the successive stages described above until it has reached the level of understanding applicable to the physical world. Because of this, we can comprehend the universe's laws, rhythms and workings by reaching out to it with human understanding. We are now using this intelligence to fashion the mineral world into many forms and structures, and while doing so either permeating these with a harmonizing aesthetic and higher purpose - or neglecting this.

But our universe was not meant to be and has not remained solely an expression of wisdom. The principles of freedom and love have entered into man's - and thus the world's - evolution. Through us, the kingdoms of nature can become imbued with love; we can shape the mineral world into forms literally built out of love rather than those simply dictated by the intellect or the will to power. The plant world, cultivated with love, will evolve in different directions than if we impose a mineralized, rationalized farming upon it. The animal world, nurtured with love, will find through us new possibilities of evolution supportive of and in harmony with man's activities and needs rather than simply being subdued to man's voracity.

The principles of love and freedom must enter into all of man's life and deeds - especially into his formative activity with the realms of nature.

---

[21] An architect can design a sitting room or garden; a computer has no room in its circuits for the life of these.

The critical question accompanying the evolution of artificial intelligence, then, is this: how do we imbue these constructions with the new principle of love? Is this possible? They will certainly carry over into future evolutions the outer form of the low-point of earthly intelligence, the intellect. This is surely part of their task: to carry out for man the repetitive functions of earthly intellect, not least in order that man himself is freed to move forward *beyond* this, to remount the steps of intelligence's fall through our own conscious and purposeful activity. But *how* we shape these beings' physical form of incarnation is of vital importance to *how* this task will be carried forward. In particular, they can be created and used in a way which leads us further down the path that then leads to the mechanization of our *own* intelligence - or they can be used to free our intelligence from a focus on mechanical tasks to enable it to find its way back to its cosmic inheritance.

We are imprinting our intellectual achievements here upon the lowest realm accessible to us, the mineral world.[22] But in doing so we face the danger of being confronted everywhere with the outer form, the hardened shell, the husk of intellect in the very world we fashion for ourselves. Only if we truly understand what we are doing here will we find the proper place for this synthetic intellect and ensure that there is still room in the world for man's human qualities: an engaged will, an active love and a living intelligence.

There are thus two challenges to meet in our confrontation with the form of artificial intelligence to be met with in computers. One is that human intelligence will be led by the mechanization of intelligence, rather than leading it. This danger is least likely to be noticed by those developing the technology, as they are least in danger of falling into a non-creative, subsidiary relation to the machinery since they best understand it and are actively creative in their work with it. What they of course often fail to comprehend is the effect of these technologies upon man's life of soul and spirit - including their own. Many of those who are most concerned with this effect, on the other hand, are unable to fully understand the technology itself. To bring an increased comprehension of both the technology and the soul and spirit realities that underlie our relationship to it is the first challenge.

But even if man preserves a healthy soul life despite his inevitable contact with computers, what of the beings that are thus incarnating into the world? In a sense there is *one* being who underlies all computer technology,

---

[22] We have full and conscious control over the mineral world. The electrical realm which we seem to manipulate in computer circuitry is actually not directly accessible to us; we can only manipulate the mineral layers to form the conditions under which the electrical realm will operate predictably.

incarnating in a manifold of individual devices. What effect does our fashioning these technological forms have on world evolution? What vessels for incarnation are we creating? This is the greater challenge, the macrocosmic one: to remain responsible for the cosmic deed we are engaged in. This is a task that will need to be carried over aeons and phases of world evolution: both to care for the world to which we are introducing a new, in many ways and levels detrimental element; and to care for the future development of these beings.

Love is active knowledge, and without real understanding there can be no love. If we can awaken in ourselves a real understanding of the nature of the beings we are working with here and of their mission; if we can even face these beings with not just understanding of but compassion for their nature and mission, then we will begin to find the ways to redeem them that cosmic evolution will also need. And if those who create new forms in this realm become capable of real understanding, knowledge and perception of what it is that they are creating, and in the face of this develop this love and compassion, then the future will be able to be looked forward to with a degree of confidence.

The beings of pure logic will be there with us in the future. They will incarnate into the forms being made available for them. But human love and the will to redeem these beings through the forces and insight developed out of an unsentimental recognition of and compassion for them may also be there in sufficient force. Upon this depends our future - and not just ours alone. Upon our insightful love and compassionate will depends the whole earth's evolution as well.

We posed the question as to what form of intelligence it is that inhabits the computer. The answer is, it is the *dead image* of intelligence, the reflection that we ourselves have put there. It is intelligence's shadow, without intelligence's light. It is an empty form, a barren shell.

We can breathe life into this mirror for moments. As soon as man steps away from in front of the devices, they return to being empty mechanisms. Looking at our creation, we see our own reflection, our own intelligence in the polished mirror we have made, and we almost believe the reflection before us to be itself imbued with life.

Outwardly - out into the heavenly spaces - there is a manifestation as of personality, a personality, however, that is not guided by an inner I, but regulated from outside like a machine.[23] So Steiner described our own existence on Saturn, our own physical bodies given the form but not yet the inner nature of personality. So are computers now; they have the outer form but not the inner reality of intelligence.

[23] Steiner, Occult Science, p. 125.

Death and Life in Modern Thinking

Jonael Schickler

In his wonderful little book, *Structural Phenomenology*, Herbert Witzenmann describes how, within the thinking process, four different stages in the life of the concept can be distinguished (See Witzenmann 1983):

(i) Its <u>actuality</u> corresponds to the moment when the thinking self grasps an idea intuitively by actualizing its pure, spiritual content. An example of this is grasping a mathematical or philosophical truth.

(ii) The <u>intentionality</u> of the concept corresponds to its capacity to reach out beyond itself as a supersensible reality towards the world of appearances. This capacity lies, for example, behind our ability to recognize new, previously unencountered instances of concepts in the world - e.g. a new species of animal.

(iii) The <u>metamorphosis</u> of the concept refers to its ability to undergo continuous change within the world of appearances whilst retaining its internal unity, as when we imagine the growth through a sequence of stages of a living organism like a plant.

(iv) A concept reaches the <u>inherence</u> level of its being when it is held fast or dies, as a single mental image, into an unchanging percept.

This is a fixed unity of concept and percept, not a gradually unfolding one. This four-fold biography of the concept within thinking is the structural archetype of the human knowledge-drama. Every self-conscious, thinking being creates the world he or she lives in by actively participating - in a way conditioned by individual temperament - in these different levels of concept individualization.[1] An accomplished artist or poet, for example, possesses a

---

[1] The historical origin of this four-foldness is Aristotle's division in <u>De Anima</u> of the human organization into a physical body (corresponding to the inherence of the concept) and vegetative, sensitive and intellectual souls (corresponding to the metamorphosis, intentionality and actuality of the concept). The epistemological version of Aristotle's ontology here considered can be seen as responding to the need to discover a structural isomorphism between thinking and being, and thus to show that the concept in the thinking act has the same internal structure as the object of knowledge. If this isomorphism were lacking, the thinker would be incapable of knowing the different levels of being to be found in the world. For example, in the absence of a correlate of dead matter within thinking (in this case the inherent concept), the mind would have no means of grasping dead matter for what it is.

thinking that lives foremost in the capacity of the concept to undergo imaginative metamorphosis; the thinking of an analytic scientist - though often motivated by intuition or imagination - by contrast, usually comes to rest in the inherence of the concept, for example in the image of a molecular structure or the state of a physical system at a particular point in time.

The principle aim of this essay is to use this four-fold biography of the concept to diagnose epistemologically the two predominant, but ideologically sharply opposed, traditions of thinking in modern university life, the analytic and the post-modern. It is divided into three sections:

(i) In the first the focus is on academic philosophy, though the distinction between analytically-oriented and post modern thinkers is to be found in many university departments, especially in the humanities.

(ii) Section two considers historically the philosophical background of the emergence during the twentieth century of these two traditions. It concentrates on the loss of the concept of the self in twentieth century philosophy.

(iii) The last section considers post-modern thought in contrast to analytical natural science. It claims that the imbalances of analytic and post-modern thinking will only be overcome if a means of knowing nature phenomenologically and not just analytically is cultivated.[2]

1. Analytical and post-modern thought[3]

A recent philosophical encyclopaedia entry on philosophical analysis defines it as "...a method of inquiry in which one seeks to assess complex systems of thought by analyzing them into simpler elements whose relationships are thereby brought into focus". (See the entry 'Analytic

---

[2] Phenomenology - the practise of systematically observing and describing phenomena or what appears within immediate consciousness - has been widely practised in the twentieth century, but predominantly outside the realm of natural science. Heidegger, for example, practised existential phenomenology, Wittgenstein a form of linguistic phenomenology, Merleau-Ponty phenomenologies of perception and the body, and depth psychologists have researched the contents of dream life phenomenologically.

[3] It is to be emphasized that the following represents a general characterization of these two traditions. 'Post-modernism' and 'analytic philosophy' are both impossible to define clearly and should be taken as, above all, different species of philosophical and spiritual temperament. (The term 'post-modernism' was initially coined in the 1950s to describe a style of architecture, but has since been appropriated as the generic term for a much more widespread cultural movement.)

Philosophy' in the *Routledge Encyclopaedia of Philosophy*.) Analytic philosophy, a largely twentieth century movement which is dominant in English and American universities, can be seen - as this definition of philosophical analysis indicates - as a cultural cousin of the positivist scientific rationalism that separates nature into its material constituents and then identifies reality with the latter.

A similar entry on post-modernism states that among the most important insights of this cultural movement are that "... the world is not One", and that "words like truth, nature, reality and even human are 'weasel' words because they imply, falsely, that an autonomous world of values and meanings exists, and that it transcends all finite and mutually exclusive human systems and somehow guarantees them. Post-modernism denies absolute status to any truth, nature or reality. The question always remains - what truth, which nature, whose reality?" (See the entry under 'Post-modernism' in the same encyclopaedia.)

Despite a few widely shared assumptions (that there is no transcendent spiritual reality, that life has no ultimate meaning...), analytic and post-modern thinking are in most respects polar opposites. Analytic thinking is philosophically conservative, and can be seen as a reactionary form of rationalist, Enlightenment thought. The philosophical problems with which most of its recent exponents struggle are - despite the 'linguistic turn' and an increased emphasis on the importance of analyzing language - largely characteristic of seventeenth and eighteenth century European philosophy.[4] Analytic philosophers take much of their philosophical inspiration from the natural sciences and mathematics. Post-modern thinking, by contrast, continues a tradition of anti-Enlightenment thought that begins soon after the death of Hegel in 1831. It tries to be philosophically revolutionary, and its most important historical sources include the writings of Marx, Freud, Nietzsche and Heidegger. Its exponents usually take a deeper interest in literature and the arts than in the natural sciences. (The post-modern movement in philosophy is French in origin.)

The simplest way of illustrating the cardinal differences between analytic (A) and post-modern (P) thinking is to summarize the way in which central philosophical concepts are typically understood in each tradition[5]:

[4] This claim will be substantiated in section two. The most important founders of analytic philosophy are Frege, the early Wittgenstein, Russell and the Logical Positivists.

[5] For each of the claims about the two traditions made in this table, there are thinkers who would defend quite different positions to the ones indicated. Its purpose is thus to sketch impressionistically the main differences between analytic and post-modern thinking.

Subject: A: Is typically identified with the physical body,
                especially the brain and the central nervous system.
                P: Is a semantic space within a web of cultural and
                linguistic practises.

Object: A: Exists independently of the human mind. Has real
                fixity.
                P: Is a mind and language-dependent process. Has no
                fixity.

Concept: A: Has been called an 'abstract object'. (This revealingly
                reflects the attempt to think of it as something finite and
                bounded.)
                P: Its movement, fluidity and subtlety of content are
                emphasized.

Truth: A: Is a property of the relationship between the meanings
                of sentences.
                P: Does not exist. There are only interpretations.

Reality: A: Is best described by the natural sciences.
                P: Is created within human practices and institutions.

Self: A: Is a grammatical fiction - i.e. a tool of language-use
                and not anything metaphysically substantial or
                fundamental.
                P: Is de-centred; the movement of differences within
                thought and feeling. The self is not the essence of reality.

Life: A: Has no ultimate meaning; was a biological accident.
                P: All meaning is created by man.

History: A: Is not relevant to a consideration of philosophical
                problems.
                P: Is a key to understanding the nature of philosophical
                questions.

World: A: Is a collection of its parts. Has no intrinsic order.
                P: Has no unity, is not One, but a constantly moving
                plurality.

It was stated in the introduction that differences like these can be diagnosed as the outcome of different structural biographies of the concept in the thinking act. How is this to be understood?

The tendency to identify reality with the results of conceptual or scientific analysis represents the elevation into the status of a worldview of the concept that has come to rest at the inherence level in the percept. The universal thinking self has passed (as thinking act) from the realm of pure universality (the pre-individualized concept) into the particular (the thinking content) in which it externalizes itself. A paradigmatic expression of this self-externalization of man achieved by analytic thinking, is the familiar existential projection of the thinking self into a vast, dark and indifferent space filled with whirling galaxies, stars and emptiness. By participating in worlds like this, the self casts itself into a dead space (the thinking content) that retains no trace of the vehicle (the thinking act) that brought it there. (This separation of the thinking act from the thinking content is the origin of the third person perspective on reality that is required for the statement of, for example, a scientific fact.)

The life of the concept characteristic of post-modern thinking is very different. It does not come to rest in something experienced as enduring and external to the thinker, but moves with restlessness and often caprice from one image or thought to another, constantly replacing old ideas with new ones. The powerful experience of the reality of change and displacement makes relativism the bosom truth of post-modern culture. Man is no longer at home in a lifeless world of objects and regular material events; he wanders homeless from one culture, language and epoch to another, constantly assimilating new distinctions and perspectives through the porous and fragile boundary of human subjectivity. Here the universal thinking self has passed through the inherence stage of the concept and is awakening to a self-conscious awareness of its capacity to undergo living metamorphosis[6]. (Such thinking emphasizes the embeddedness of the third person perspective in the content of first person experience.)

Analytic and post-modern thinking can thus be shown to represent two very different types of life within thought, each of which issues in a different characteristic picture of the world. The fluidity, immanence and extreme subtlety of much post-modern thinking is a clear sign of the beginnings of a cultural transition from the consciousness characteristic of scientific rationalism towards more participatory forms of knowing. However, the reactionary presence of a conservative analytic tradition in philosophy testifies to the enormous resistance that this transition is encountering.

---

[6] In anthroposophical terminology, this reflects a culture that has passed through the reality of physical thinking into a thinking that 'lives more self-consciously in the movement of the etheric.

Within post-modern thinking itself this resistance manifests as a persistent underlying current of materialism and secularism that, despite its efforts to free itself from reductive and rationalist thinking, still invades the delicate post-modern mind.[7]

A diagnosis of the two dominant intellectual cultures of contemporary academia must examine their historical background. The next section briefly attempts to do so by considering how each stands to the philosophical discoveries of the German Idealists, and particularly to the concept of the self.

2. The historical background

Both analytic and post-modern thought have intricate and many-stranded histories. If there is one location in the territory of philosophical discourse, however, where an overlap between them can be discovered, it is the philosophy of Kant. Kant introduced the concept of the transcendental subject into philosophical thought.[8] This subject is the universal 'I think' whose synthetic activity causes things in the world to appear to us as objects with properties by constituting them as such through the thinking act. Objectivity as we encounter it (the presence to consciousness of an inter-subjectively accessible world of objects) is on this view the result of human thought; it does not consist in a state of the world beyond the thinking act.[9] His philosophical achievements allowed Kant to claim that experienced reality is simultaneously empirically real and objective (it can be known and studied...) and transcendentally ideal (its experienced form is due to the conceptual apparatus of the human subject). Kant called his transcendental idealism a Copernican revolution in philosophy, because in his system the world conforms to the thinking self, whereas in previous modern systems (e.g. those of Locke, Leibniz and Spinoza) the world had conformed to the object.[10]

[7] I have known thinkers heavily influenced by post-modernist authors like Deleuze, Foucault and Derrida to identify themselves with what they call 'non-metaphysical materialism'. The latter is supposed to be more refined than metaphysical materialism because it upholds a fluid and linguistically relativist, rather than a static and scientifically realist conception of matter. It is, in other words, a confused materialism of the metamorphosis of the concept.

[8] It is transcendental since it is a condition of the possibility of the experienced world, rather than something within that world.

[9] Kant defines the object as "the unity of intuitions [or percepts] within a concept".

[10] Aristotle's philosophy contains an early version of the idea that the thinking self, not the object, lies at the centre of reality. He claimed that the human being possesses a creative intellectual soul (nous poietikos), which is the 'thinking that makes all things', and a receptive intellectual soul (nous pathetikos), the 'thinking that becomes all things'. The former, as thinking act, creates the content that is apprehended by the latter. (See De Anima, Book 3

Kant's Idealist successors, Fichte, Schelling and Hegel, elaborated and challenged his conclusions in profound ways in trying to complete the revolution they considered him to have begun but, as an epistemological sceptic, had failed to see through to its conclusion. (His scepticism consists in the view that knowledge can be only of appearances, not of the reality - or thing in itself - that lies behind them.) By the time we reach Hegel's dialectical philosophy, for example, the dualisms and last vestiges of the onlooker consciousness (for which reality is given and complete outside the subject) that still beset Kant's thinking and that were the defining feature of post-Cartesian rationalist and empiricist philosophy, have been left behind.[11]

So how does Kant provide a link in the polarity between analytic and post-modern thinking?

The central questions that analytic philosophers are concerned with are the very questions that Kant's philosophy claimed to have answered or rendered obsolete with the introduction of the transcendental subject. Yet whenever an analytic philosopher studies Kant, it is precisely the presence of this concept that causes him to take a step backwards towards a philosophical position more characteristic of pre-Kantian thought (see e.g. McDowell 1994). This represents a retreat towards a worldview consonant with the ethos of natural science and its onlooker consciousness; for as soon as the transcendental subject - the omnipresent 'I think' of a human world - is taken seriously, it becomes increasingly difficult for a thinker attempting

---

[10/ contd] chapter 5.) This intellectual soul is transformed, in modernity, into the thinking self. Perhaps the cardinal difference between the philosophy of antiquity and that of modernity, is that with the awakening of the self, a concept enters into philosophical and everyday discourse that is capable of yielding a logically complete account of the relationship between man (the finite self) and God (the infinite self), so satisfying the intrinsic monotheistic impulses of the rational intellect. (In Aristotle's philosophy this relationship remains unresolved.) This logical completeness is to be found in an understanding of the nature of self-consciousness and particularly its reflexivity - the unity within consciousness of a self as subject (I) and a self as object (Me), and their logical inter-dependence. (See Hegel (2) and Steiner Philosophie u. Anthroposophie, p. 102 for examples of thought that capitalizes on the latent internal logic of the linguistically isolated first person pronoun.)

[11] Hegel's Phenomenology of Spirit, in particular, describes with breathtaking logic and depth a path taken by the self through different forms of consciousness towards what he called a state of absolute knowing, in which all dualisms - epistemological, existential, moral... - have been overcome. Here the many different types of experience self-consciousness has, whether as a member of society or as an inquirer into nature etc., of a reality that exists beyond the self, are seen as different ways in which the self as subject (the universal 'I') knows itself as object (e.g. as a monk, a biological organism, a king...) before it reaches the state in which it knows the identity of the self as subject and the self as object. (Philosophies that have the concept of the self at their centre, such as those of the Idealists and Steiner, represent the elevation into the status of a worldview of the concept's actuality.)

to overcome Kant's scepticism to circumvent the idea that the purely spiritual self is the creative centre and ultimate substance of reality (a conclusion eagerly latched on to by the Idealists who followed Kant). So long as natural scientific realism is culturally dominant, the idea of finding in the thinking self that vital link between man (microcosm) and the world (macrocosm) is for most unthinkable. Hence the recoil within much academic philosophy to anaemic and often pedantic reflection on the problems of the onlooker consciousness.

Post-modern thinking can be related to Kant from the opposite perspective. Mindful of the metaphysical monism that one is driven to if Kant's Copernican revolution is completed, post-modernists follow in a tradition of post-Hegelian thinkers like Nietzsche, Heidegger and the later Wittgenstein, who deny the very possibility of the rationalist philosophy (dominant from Aristotle to Hegel), in which pure thought attempts to grasp the unified internal logic of the world. Post-modernists thus also retreat from the idea that the human self is the unfolding epicentre of reality, but do so in the direction of a decentralized, fragmented and historically relativist conception of the human condition. Such thinking is anti-rationalist in the extreme since it rejects the possibility of discovering in the self, or indeed in any other concept, a means of uniting man with reality as a whole. In his efforts to discover fresh avenues for the life of thought, the post-modernist attempts to overcome the inevitable unity into which the rationalist must think reality by rejecting the concept of self entirely, instead of cultivating a new understanding of it as did, for example, Nietzsche and Steiner.[12]

Kant sits squarely between analytic and post-modern thought to the extent that he is the originator of the philosophical movement that led to the discovery of the spiritual self within Western thinking, the self-creating 'I'

---

[12] In Nietzsche's Thus Spoke Zarathustra, the self is identified with the human body: "Behind your thoughts and feelings, my brother, stands a mighty commander, an unknown sage - he is called Self. He lives in your body, he is your body. There is more reason in your body than in your best wisdom..." Steiner echoes and deepens Nietzsche's statement through the thought that the human physical body is the most complete of the four principle members of man's being, and that human freedom is attained when the self of human consciousness, the totally universal yet also intimately individual 'I', is finally united in godliness (as Atman) with the spiritual beings whose symphonic activity comes to rest in the finite vessel of man's strivings. Steiner thus reveals Nietzsche's unknown sage, the self of the body, to be a harmonious chorus of spiritual beings, with Christ - who unified them by resurrecting a physical body as a higher self - at their head. This achievement represents the fulfilment of the aims of the German Idealists since it unites the two poles of man's being, the self and the physical body, and in so doing shows how the transcendental subject becomes fully immanent.

that twentieth century philosophy and culture felt compelled to abandon.[13] Much remains to be said about the loss of the self in twentieth century thought, and about how thinkers like Heidegger and Wittgenstein (both closely related to Kant intellectually) attempted to practise philosophy without many of its traditional concepts - and what influence this had on their successors in post-modern and analytic philosophy. However, this is not the place for such a detailed discussion.

The origin of the separation of philosophy into the analytic and post-modern traditions is thus intimately intertwined with different cultural reactions against the central status of the concept of self (and its 'logocentrism'[14]). To an outsider these traditions, which to their detriment have also made themselves into small publishing industries, can seem like two increasingly obscure and irrelevant tributaries of a cultural river whose turbulent and polluted waters threaten to carry the mass of humanity into the abyss of nihilism - an abyss of which both analytic and post-modern philosophy are, to the extent that they uphold materialistic values, ultimately guardians.

The following section considers how a widely practised phenomenology of nature might be capable of bringing calm and renewed life to the disturbed waters of modern culture, by demonstrating the possibility of integrating scientific rationalism with more imaginative forms of thinking. A crucial outcome of these consideration will be a new position for the concept of self.

3. A phenomenology of nature

The analytic approach to understanding nature is intrinsically reductionist, for it attempts to find a reality in nature that exists behind the world of appearances, rather than in and through them.[15] It does so by representing nature in homogeneous, universalizing terms, considering natural phenomena in abstraction and as the sum of their parts. The post-modern

[13] In light of the social and political upheavals of the past century, anything other than such an abandonment is difficult to conceive. The forces that were unleashed on humanity during the Second World War in particular represent a tragic and passively suffered subversion of the self-legislating individual subject. Any spiritually ambitious philosophy of the self contemporary with National Socialism, for example, would thus have been culturally meaningless.

[14] Any attempt to think the whole reflects what Derrida called 'logocentrism', and is treated with immediate suspicion by the post-modernist.

[15] The law of nature as conventionally conceived, for example, is considered as a one-over-many (i.e. identically instantiated under all conditions) rather than as a one-in-many (in every instance uniquely individualized).

conception of nature, on the other hand, is influenced predominantly by semantic, historical and anthropological considerations. It emphasizes that the concept of nature has different meanings in different times, contexts and cultures, and that the natural world is experienced, interpreted and manipulated in accordance with instrumental social and cultural (e.g. religious) ends. The analytical approach thus tends to dehumanize and de-spiritualize nature, the post-modern approach to denaturalize it.

It was suggested above that nature as understood within orthodox natural science reflects knowledge of the level of being that corresponds to the inherence of the concept, where the latter is held fast in the percept.[16] It was also claimed that the relativism intrinsic to post-modern thinking reflects the concept's capacity to undergo metamorphosis. The task of a phenomenology of nature is to unite the cognitive tendencies of these traditions by discovering the level of being in nature that corresponds to the metamorphosis of the concept. This is achieved by a thinking that, as a result of careful observation and imaginative effort, is able to participate in the wholeness or what Bortoft has called the 'intensive depth' and Adams and Whicher the 'inner infinitude' of phenomena (see Bortoft 1996 and Adams and Whicher 1982).

The most significant feature of a thinking that actualizes the capacity of the concept to undergo metamorphosis, is that it lives in recognition of the truth that living wholes are extended not only through space (the inherence of the concept) but also through time (its metamorphosis). As such it complements the thinking of orthodox natural science, where the object is represented as already given in its nature (and thus as something already past rather than present) before the thinker comes into contact with it (see Goethe 1981 , Adams and Whicher 1982, and Bockemühl 1977 for examples of such thinking in connection with the plant kingdom).

Modern science does work with concepts (for example the field in physics) that could be thought of as corresponding to the level of being of which the metamorphosis of the concept is the epistemological correlate. However, the failure to cultivate methods of knowing that grasp such entities as the morphic or morphogenetic fields of living organisms through immediate experience has meant that scientists have used concepts that elude the analytic mode of thinking (see Goodwin 1994 and Sheldrake 1988). Many post-modern thinkers, by contrast, have begun practising more fluid, imaginative and less systematic forms of thinking (especially as

---

[16] To construe the physical body as a molecular system, for example, is to identify it with a set of concept-percept unities or representations at the inherence level of the concept.

researchers into the arts and literature), but have failed to apply them to an understanding of nature.[17]

Perhaps the most significant reason why neither tradition has been able to extend its methodological principles in the direction of the other (quite apart from the stifling ideological presuppositions on which each rests), is that each has largely taken flight from the world of the senses. The analytical scientist feeds increasingly off a diet of technical terms and mathematical formalism, while the post-modernist draws much of his sustenance from elaborate metaphors and heaven-bound poetic imagery. In contrast to this, phenomenology of nature demands that direct attention should be paid to what can be observed without technical aids or theoretical schemas. To use a theatrical analogy, the phenomenologist reads the spiritual content of nature from the language and gestures of the play itself - be it the drama of plant life or animal morphology (see Schad 1977) - rather than from its mechanically functioning stage props, allowing the former to explain the latter. Opposed to this the hard sciences tell us not to trust our senses in making judgements about the nature of reality, while the post-modernist constantly emphasizes that the sensory present is infused with semantic 'traces' (Derrida) of the cultural past.[19]

This departure from the reality of the senses is reflected within analytic philosophy itself (as well as amongst theoretical scientists) by those who claim (as does for example the philosopher of science Feyerabend) that the scientific theoretician's models of reality should not be taken as describing the truth about the world, since they are merely constructions in the minds of men. The symptom within post-modern thought of the same malaise is the widespread claim that human life is no more than the expression of personal and cultural narratives or stories that humans construct for themselves. Reality thus becomes a form of fiction, it becomes

[17] Heidegger's philosophy reflects a very deep understanding of the need to develop non-theoretical forms of thinking that enable the life of thought to participate in the richness of Being. But the phenomenological method that he cultivated (Being and Time, Heidegger's magnum opus, is a work of existential phenomenology - i.e. phenomenology of the human life-world of everyday existence) was never applied directly (as was Goethe's method) to the natural world, and this set the tone for his many post-modern successors.

[18] For Derrida the present becomes "the sign of signs, the trace of traces" (Derrida 1973).

[19] Insofar as the post-modern thinker historicizes the sensory present, and the analyst rigidly fixes it, both lose contact with the living forms that operate in perceived reality. (One only needs to observe the absorption in its surroundings of the child to regain a sense for what participation in nature could be for the receptive mind.) This loss represents what Nietzsche called 'unfaithfulness to the earth', because within the earth form and matter exist as a unity, and where thinking loses the sensory present to a world of abstractions (a Nietzschean example would be the passive expectation of an afterlife), it no longer experiences this unity.

virtual. Both the 'model' and the 'story', however, are concepts that in ordinary language are used to distinguish the unreal from reality (and, as Hegel pointed out, ordinary language contains an implicit worldview - reflecting the progress made by the *Weltgeist* - that is often wiser than man!). Each thus reaffirms in its own way the man-world dualism that is the *idée fixe* of modern thought.

The challenge, then, is to know nature at the level of being that corresponds to the metamorphosis of the concept - as alive with creative formative forces. Again, there is insufficient space here to develop this thought in any detail. Suffice it to say that though significant advances have been made in realizing such a science of the living as living (a science of the etheric - see Marti 1989 and Thomas 1999 for two very different attempts to develop the idea of a science of the etheric[20]), a tremendous amount of work remains to be done, particularly in understanding how ethers and formative forces (the two-dimensional entities that, according to Steiner, occupy the space of the etheric) are active in nature and how they can be understood in a way capable of extending orthodox modern science.

It was claimed above that a phenomenology of nature is capable of returning to philosophical culture the concept of the self. A science of the etheric, however, would still fall far short of knowledge of the levels of being that correspond to the intentionality and actuality of the concept,[21] and it is in the world of the latter that the self is ultimately at home. The question can, however, be looked at from another perspective. A culture that awakens to the reality of the etheric (the thinking of post-modernists can, at its best, be seen as a symptom of such an awakening), would be one that has passed through the death that European culture suffered in the first half of the twentieth century. For wherever death is self-consciously overcome (as when we overcome existential crises, or when the thinker resurrects imaginatively concepts that have died into percepts), it is a new self that emerges on the other side.

The self that must emerge (and in places is emerging) out of the dark events of the twentieth century into a living grasp of the etheric is a self that has learned to live in a more intimate and participatory relationship with its dynamically evolving world. Unlike the self of German Idealist thought it recognizes the great extent of its own passivity in the face of the major occurrences of human history (as well as its own biography), for it knows most human consciousness to be the surface of events whose ultimate causes

[20] In his <u>Das Ätherische</u>   E. Marti attempts to explain the differences between ethers and formative forces.

[21] In anthroposophical terminology, the astral and spiritual (Devachan) worlds.

lie at levels of being far beyond the cognitive reach of ordinary human experience.[22] This self thus also recognizes the limits of the rational intellect (or self) that attempts, as did Hegel in particular, to think the whole. Yet it does so without thereby feeling the need to reject the extraordinary discoveries - so brilliantly present in the synthetic dialectic of a work like Hegel's *Science of Logic* - that this intellect is capable of making.

Conclusion

The widespread practice of a phenomenology of nature would represent, for the sciences, entry into a whole new stage in the biography of the concept, one capable of releasing the modern thinker from the heavy yoke of materialistic nihilism. It would also free disciplines like philosophy from the paternalistic presence of the natural sciences, allowing the cultivation of imaginatively rich forms of thinking whose validity is recognized within the cultural milieu as a whole.

The origins of the corrosive duality that lies at the heart of today's academy are complex and many-sided. Epistemologically, analytic and post-modern thought can be diagnosed by situating the forms of thinking that they express within a set of possibilities defined by the fundamental structural features of the thinking process. Historically, they are best considered in relation to the philosophical achievements of Kant and the German Idealists, for each represents an implicit reaction against the centralizing tendencies of those idealistic philosophies that have the characteristically modern concept of the self at their apex.

Both traditions are perhaps best understood more generally in relation to the extraordinary achievements of the natural sciences in this century. The often destructive extremity of the post-modern critique of Enlightenment rationality can sound above all like the frustrated cry of an ailing society incapable of generating a flourishing spiritual and artistic centre able to balance the heady prestige of the current scientific worldview. The lifeless pedantry of excessively analytic thinking, on the other hand, conveys a sullen resignation before the thought that in the face of the successes of the 'hard sciences', philosophy is a distinctly secondary, if not a dead subject.

If a non-materialistic understanding of nature does not become widespread, there is a very real danger that the seeds of a cultural renewal that were sown upon European soil through Steiner's work (itself the fruit of Europe's cultural flowering a hundred years previously) will fail to germinate and bring about the spiritual rejuvenation, the new life within thinking, that our dying culture so desperately needs.[23]

[22] The highly significant discoveries of depth psychologists (like Stanislav Grof) in especially the second half of the twentieth century reflect research that has taken this thought to heart. It has been claimed (by R. Tarnas, for example - see his The Passion of the Western Mind) that depth psychology represents the true continuation of the spiritual impulses alive in the thought of figures like Hegel and Steiner. Depth psychology (whose founders were Freud and Jung) would represent a third philosophically important cultural movement of the twentieth century. Its influence, however, has not - psycho-analysis excepted - extended significantly into the university arena.

[23] The four-foldness introduced at the beginning of the text can be developed in many different ways. The following schema, based on Steiner's work, might help the reader to think through more of these and their relationships to one another independently:

Concept:	Actuality	Intentionality	Metamorphosis	Inherence
Man:	Self	Astral body	Etheric body	Physical body
Time:	Super-temporal	Future	Present	Past
Space:	Point (0-D)	Line (1-D)	Plane (2-D)	Solid (3-D)
Elements:	Fire	Air	Water	Earth
Ethers:	Warmth	Light	Sound/chemical	Life
Cognition:	Intuition	Inspiration	Imagination	Self-consciousness

References:

Adams and Whicher. *The Plant Between Sun and Earth,* Boulder 1982.

Aristotle. *De Anima.* The Complete Works of Aristotle - revised Oxford translation, Princeton 1984.

Bockemühl, J. 'The Formative Movements of Plants' in *Towards a Phenomenology of the Etheric World,* Stuttgart 1977.

Bortoft, H. *The Wholeness of Nature - Goethe's Way of Science.* Edinburgh 1996.

Derrida, J. *Speech and Phenomena, and Other Essays on Husserl's Theory of Signs.* Evanston Ill. 1973.

Goethe. *Die Metamorphose der Pflanze,* Werke - Hamburger Ausgabe 1981, Band 13.

Goodwin, B. *How the Leopard Changed its Spots*, London 1994.

Hegel, G.W.F.

    (1) *Phänomenologie des Geistes* (Meiner Verlag), Hamburg 1988.

    (2) *Wissenschaft der Logik II,* Hamburg 1986

Heidegger, *Being and Time.* Oxford 1962.

Marti, E. *Das Ätherische.* Dornach 1989.

McDowell, J. *Mind and World,* Cambridge, Mass. 1994.

Nietzsche, F. *Thus Spoke Zarathustra,* London 1961.

Routledge Encyclopaedia of Philosophy, London 1999.

Sheldrake, R. *The Presence of the Past.* London 1988.

Steiner, R. *Anthroposophie und Philosophie.*

Thomas, N. *Science between Space and Counterspace.* London 1999.

Witzenmann, H: *Strukturphänomenologie,* Dornach 1983.

Awakening to the history of the Anthroposophical movement and the Society[1]

Bodo von Plato

Translated by William B. Forward

What is living in the historical process, and how to recognise it

How can a preoccupation with history become meaningful, and to what end, if it is to go beyond a mere middle-class obsession with education? Wherein lies and lives the primary concern of history?

This must be the human being and the forces that determine his actions and development; the human being in his relation to himself and to others in space and time. The driving forces behind history, not the facts themselves, live in a sphere which is inaccessible to a way of thinking that is exclusively concerned with those facts. The unfolding of history can be perceived by the human being in a state of consciousness which is comparable to that of dreaming. "What is at work in the process of history passes through the human soul no more clearly, nor indeed differently, than a dream. It is perfectly scientific to speak of the dream of human becoming."[2]

Historical facts are like the tracks left behind by the progress of history. In and of themselves they have nothing to say, and yet if they are linked in a causal sequence, they lead one astray into preconceived images and ideas. Historical facts relate to the living process of history as the corpse of a human being relates to his living soul.

There can be a variety of motives and aims behind the contemplation of history. They may lie at the root of our consideration of history, often unwittingly so, rather in the same sort of relationship that the individual human being in everyday life has to himself, to his own process of becoming, ie. to himself as an historical being.There follows a brief characterisation of some of the more common approaches and of one which is rather less commonly adopted.

History as progress towards salvation. The assumption is that a divine or spiritual providence is manifest in all that appears in the process of becoming, in history itself. All historical processes, including one's own biography, it is assumed, are directed towards a particular goal. All that takes place on the way to this goal is ultimately interpreted as a manifestation of a divine, spiritual, or at least superior will. Salvation consciousness lives in the view, the assumption or even the desire to demonstrate that there is a divine, spiritual or superior necessity. Such a consciousness was cultivated in the Christian Middle Ages, by Marxist-Leninists and is so by believers in a whole variety of cultural or spiritual movements.

History as self portrayal. This involves the portrayal of a particular form of existence -- an epoch, a style of life, a figure or a person - by means of historical facts. Events are arranged and represented in such a way that the form emerges which one has selected according to a preconceived idea, ideal, wish or directive. The aim is self-affirmation, the representation of one's own point of view or person. This approach is often adopted by the historians of a ruling class or others seeking to legitimise their position, but may also underlie some forms of psychological practice and opinion-forming on current affairs.

History as teacher. Events in the past are studied in order to draw lessons from them for one's actions in the present or future. Past experiences, whether social or personal, are examined with a view to avoiding the repetition of mistakes or undesirable developments. Whilst it is essential for conscious development that one draws lessons from the past, the benefits of such a study are limited by the fact that experiences cannot be transferred and that forces or ideas seldom reappear in the same garb. The destructive power and contempt for humanity, for instance, which lived in National Socialism, are unlikely to reappear in the guise of brown uniforms and racist or biologically deterministic attitudes. It is also true that the experiences of fathers and mothers can rarely be transferred to their children.

History as a judge or weapon. Past events are evaluated against a moral yardstick, usually one based on or in the present, to determine whether they are true or false, good or bad, beautiful or ugly. Such evaluation of past situations or behaviour serves to condemn or excuse those involved, to determine innocence or guilt. A morally based analysis of history will often be used to confirm, account for, or apparently objectivise one's own position in a current conflict. Sensational revelations and tales of conflict also belong in the repertoire of this approach which has much in common with the attitude adopted in self-justification in personal conflicts or conflicts between individuals.

History as a path of self-knowledge. This is an attitude which is not often adopted when forming a relationship to the sequence of events on earth.

The moment self-knowledge and self-transformation become the primary objective in the analysis of the past, what has been moves into the background and what is in the process of becoming takes the foreground. What has been, the traces left by the process of becoming, serves as a means of awakening to the forces at work in a process of becoming, forces which may need strengthening or damping down. The future moves into the foreground as soon as one looks into the past with the attitude of one seeking for self-knowledge. This mind-set is interested in the past in order to to discover and grasp within it developmental processes which work on into the present - as forces, not as facts or pictures - and which will play a part in shaping the future. Such a consciousness will have empathy and understanding as its underlying maxims.

One can summarise these examples of possible attitudes towards the events of the past in the form of three tendencies:

A study of history in order to prove one is right: *a moralistic approach to the past.*

A study of history in order to take appropriate action in the present: *a utilitarian approach to the past.*

A study of history in order to understand the present and the future: *a history of developmental processes, or a developmental approach to the past.*

The classic question "What has been? What happened?" remains the foundation of any developmental history in the sense defined above. But an attitude that seeks and researches developmental processes goes beyond this to questions such as:"To what am I awakening? In what direction is a/my transformation taking place?" Thus the questions arising from the developmental approach lead not only to an enhanced understanding, but also to the emergence of individual impulses, to the unfolding of a guiding developmental force which is latent in every act of knowledge. In the end they become a driving force in the context of an individually directed inner schooling.

The conditions applying to research on the historical process

Three of the many methodical parameters which apply to research on the historical process are highlighted below by way of example:

The hermeneutic problem. Processes of development are only open to scrutiny to the extent that the researcher knows and transforms himself in a way that is appropriate to the object of study. Only someone who is in a process of becoming can recognize what is becoming. Only someone who is himself developing can research a process of development. The researcher can exclude himself neither from the process of research nor from its result. In his apprehension of a process of development he mirrors himself, and it is particularly his own peculiar attitude to what is past and what is still in the process of becoming which is reflected.

The problem of forming a judgement. No process of reseach can abstain from coming to conclusions. In the social realm however - in contrast to the realm of Nature and research into Nature - the judgment of the individual is always wrong or at least inadequate. The forming of an objectively true judgment, independent of the observer, is simply impossible in the case of human affairs and human relationships. This does not mean that one can avoid making judgments, but it does mean that when one is involved in forming judgements on the historical process, one wil always have to be aware of the temporary nature of such conclusions, continually have to reveal the basis on which the judgments were formed, and be prepared to change the point of view from which conclusions were drawn.

At the boundaries of knowledge. Research into history as a developmental process is always carried out empirically. In so doing one rapidly encounters contradictions which one will neither seek to explain away, nor overemphasize, for within them human life evolves in acordance with the peculiarities of each individual. Out of a conscious experience of these contradictions arises a kind of knowledge drama: "This is as far as human knowledge can reach, one cannot go any further......What matters is this: to be able to stand before such questions with all one's powers of soul, and then to refrain from using one's conceptual understanding, but rather to live with them and have patience, to wait and to see if perhaps some revelation will come to one from outside. And this does indeed happen.....Life must move on from there! And it can do so. This is something one simply has to experience." The researcher into history as development experiences as a fact of his own life something which, as he crosses a boundary of knowledge, throws him back on himself or indeed ahead to himself in his own life.

In *self knowledge and self transformation, in flexible judgment-forming and in living at the boundaries of knowledge,* the process of researching history as development will discover both its preconditions and its aims in terms of attitude and activity.

Parallels in the development of the Anthroposophical Society and the history of the twentieth century

Their understanding of the major events of the last few centuries leads present-day historians to speak of the long 19th century (from the French revolution of 1789 to the first World War of 1914/18) in contrast to the short 20th century (from the first World War of 1914/18 to the fundamental political, social and cultural changes which took effect towards the end of the Eighties and the beginning of the Nineties). According to this time-scale we have already been living in the 21st century for some years now.[4]

At the beginning of the 21st century in this sense , Yehudi Menuhin was asked how he viewed the past century and replied: "If I were to sum up the 20th century, I would say that it raised the greatest expectations ever held by the human race, and destroyed all illusions and ideals."[5]

Among the great hopes that were cherished at the beginning of the 20th century were the prospect of technical development, which would liberate humanity from material constraints, and social development, which enable humanity to live in freedom, peace and mutual respect. Today we can see that technical developments have in fact made available unprecedented potential for destruction, some of which has been exercised, and that never before has there been a comparable level of contempt shown for humanity as in the 20th century.

Anthroposophy appeared in the world at the turn of the 20th century, and it too raised far-reaching hopes for the future. These are based on the realisation of a fundamental change of paradigm, the aim of which is that human lives be shaped "both individually and socially on the basis of a true knowledge of the spiritual world."[6] Today it is apparent that the overcoming of materialism and agnosticism to any significant degree has not been a developmental feature of the 20th century. The feeling that all ideals and illusions have been destroyed may be experienced equally by the concerned observer of the events of the 20th century and the person who is reviewing the attempts that have been made to realize Anthroposophy over the past eight decades.

In simplified and highly abstract terms one can distinguish four phases in the history of the 20th century and also in that of the Anthroposophical movement since the 1920's. In doing so one should note that this is bound to involve a certain oversimplification and one should thus beware of reading too much into it, rather treating the characterisation as symptomatic.

The observations set out overleaf are based on purely superficial parallels. Glancing over them one may find that spontaneous associations point in the direction of inner links between the developments in each column; the question as to whether there is indeed such an inner correlation will require further, detailed research - what follows may be seen as a stimulus or provisional hypothesis for such research.

I. From the mid-20s to the mid-40s:

General trends (from a European perspective)	Anthroposophical movement/Society[7]
Rise and expansion of Fascism in Europe;	Leading anthroposophists fail to communicate with each other;
Crisis in world economy;	Independent practical applications of Anthroposophy attempted;
Dictatorships - National Socialism determines the fate first of Europe, then the world;	Leadership in question and in crisis;
World War;	Differentiation (1935/1942);
Genocide.	Inner and outer paralysis.

Relationship of the Anthroposophical Society to the areas of practically applied Anthroposophy and public perception of both: The significance of the Anthroposophical Society is in the foreground and its ups and downs have a lasting impact on the work of the practical applications. No impact on the public at large.

II. From the mid-40s to the mid-60s:

Post-war reconstruction and economic miracle;	Growth in the Society and practical applications, stagnation from the mid-50s;
East - West polarity;	Growth of the institutions;
Cold War;	Polarisation of different groups within the Society, consolidation at the beginning of the 60s;

Relationship of the Anthroposophical Society to the areas of practically applied Anthroposophy, and public perception of both: The Society becomes more remote and less significant as the areas of practical work strengthen and diversify. Scarcely any impact on the public at large.

III. From the mid-60s to the mid-80s

Increasing internationalisation; 1968 student movement;	New generation setting the agenda;
The alternative movement; Psychedelia;	Rapid expansion of the practical work and increase in publications;
Scepticism towards technology and increased ecological awareness;	Differentiation of function in the various areas of work;
Terrorism;	
Post-modernism;	Increasing internationalisation;
New Age movement. Science.	Re-enlivened School of Spiritual Science.

Relationship of the Anthroposophical Society to the areas of practically applied Anthroposophy, and the public perception of both: Further loss of influence for the Anthroposophical Society, while the anthroposophical work in pedagogy, medecine and agriculture becomes better known to the public at large.

IV. Since the mid - 80s

Technology applied to virtually all areas of life together with large-scale dissolution of traditional forms of life; Reduction in East - West tension, "pax americana"; Sceptical attitude towards ideologies; Pragmatism rules; Globalisation and general acceptance of post-modernist "anything goes" ethic as evidence of boundaries breaking down; fundamental restructuring of society.

Slowdown in the expansion of practical applications; Alarming absence of new generation and fall-off in membership; Sober new attitude or pessimism in regard to comprehensive renewal of civilisation and visions of the future; Quest for a new approach to Rudolf Steiner; Increased willingness to learn, self-criticism, but also hypercritical attitude; latent anthroposophical agnosticism; quest for individualised life-styles and ways of working.

Relationship of the Anthroposophical Society to the areas of practical application and public perception of both: Attempts at reorientation and renewal of the relationship. Waldorf schools, biodynamic agriculture and anthroposophical medecine occupy niches in public perception with predominantly positive connotations.

The destruction of ideals and illusions, whether in regard to the general trend of developments in the 20th century, or in regard to the prospects for a culturally effective spiritual realism, need not be seen , as might at first seem appropriate, as an entirely bad thing. It might very possibly encourage not only an attitude of resignation, but also a more reaslistic assessment of the situation in general and of the potential of individuals in particular. It might even give people more courage to discover and achieve their individual tasks.

Awakening to impulses

Where historical research leads to results and views which can, and must, be discussed in terms of their assumptions, their relative merits and their values, research into history as a process of development leads beyond this to an awakening. What one awakens to, however, is not something that can be discussed, since the awakening does not lead in the first instance to points of view, but rather manifests itself in the from of intentions, it finds expression in individual impulses. These in turn may be seen in attitudes or yearnings, in questions, in the style or direction of one's attention, in capacities, initiatives and activities, in sum: in the current reality of life.

I should like to give an account of one such impulse to which I was led after concerning myself with the history of the Anthroposophical movement and Society since 1925 against the background of remarks made by Rudolf Steiner during the period in which esoteric work was built up after the Christmas conference of 1924.

It was an impulse to transform three phenomena which are, were, and will continue to be significant in human intercourse and in particular for a spiritually oriented common striving in the Anthroposophical movement and Society: to transform *authority, criticism and communication.*

The transformation of authority. At the beginning of the 20th century a kind of socially evolved, legitimised authority and the hierarchies that arose within it still continued to work on in society as a factor that provided form and order. It was still fairly clear who was in authority, in what way and where, also how one was expected to relate to this authority. Particularly in esoteric life it played a decisive role. Today authority has degenerated to an anonymous power, or it is perceived - quite rightly, from the point of view of individualism - as an affront. The question is, how can its form-giving and directing power now come to expression in a transformed way?

It is clear, for example, from remarks Rudolf Steiner made in a course for young doctors in 1924, how, and in what direction an attitude of life that is geared to authority may be transformed. He was speaking about the role of spiritual striving in relation to a medical practice of the future, and pointed out that the esoteric life in the Anthroposophical movement up to that time had failed, for the reason that all concerned were willing to deal with him, but not with anyone else. He urged the young doctors firstly to energetically study spiritual science, and secondly to place their complete trust in Ita Wegman.[8]

Instead of looking up to authority for guidance, or of rejecting it on principle, the person who is evolving towards freedom can study spiritual science, and at the same time placehis trust in others. He thus begins to *take his fellow human beings seriously,* for what they are.

In summary, one can discern a transformation sequence:

Authority - study of spiritual science - trusting and taking one's fellow human beings seriously.

The transformation of criticism. It no longer requires any great effort for our contemporaries to identify and criticize the imperfections, onesidedness and errors of others or of their actions. The ability to criticize, which only developed into a general and widespread capacity during the 20th century, is regarded by modern culture as an expression of independence and autonomy. What is not always noticed, however, is that criticism is exercised virtually automatically, generally on the basis of sympathy or antipathy. It has a destructive, or at least paralysing effect on any effort to shape or do something which is new or the result of individual initiative, and which is not rooted in the security of tradition.

At the end of the curative education course in 1924, Rudolf Steiner spoke of the relationship of this new field of work with the refounded Anthroposophical Society. In a kind of "laying of the foundation stone", he put it to the curative teachers that it would be impossible for the Anthroposophical movement to bring forth what was "essential" in its task unless criticism of the work of others - and in particular of those carrying responsibility - were stopped.[9]

Already in 1918 he had described it as "the most beautiful and significant social skill for the future" if "one were to be able to develop a scientific, objective interest in the faults of other people, so that one would be much more inclined to take an interest in other people's faults than to try to criticize them", and if one were to concern oneself with "the other person's failings in an increasingly loving way"[10] . This would result in a *positivity,* which would make it possible for one to take sufficient interest in the other person to go beyond the necessary isolation of the individual which belongs to the age of the consciousness soul to forms of life, community and society which would be based on, and encourage, individualism.

Thus a second transformation sequence:

Criticism - scientific interest in the faults of others - positivity.

The transformation of communication. As a result of the disappearance of reliable and appropriate forms of human intercourse as the consciousness soul progresses, and of increasing individualisation, communication is becoming an increasingly important, and at the same time problematic issue. It should come as no surprise that one of the most important aspects , if not the most important aspects of modern civilisation is communications technology. Nowhere is the speed of innovation greater than in this area. Whether, and if so how, real human encounter , interest in one another or awakening to the other are in fact encouraged by this, is another question. In any case, meetings between people, and conversations between them belong to the areas of experimentation in which important things will be decided for the future of human culture. In his "Letters to members " in 1924 , Rudolf Steiner drew attention to the fundamental conditions of spiritual forms of life which would have to be observed, tried and tested in the everyday practice of running an Anthroposophical Society. This practice consists in the way in which its tasks and activities are conducted. As a result, the way in which those who are carrying them out interact plays a critical role. Rudolf Steiner observed that these active members - or, as he called them "members who wish to be active" - did not express how they felt about the activity of those working with them at the various gatherings or meetings where they exchanged views about Society business. " It would be essential that the impulse given at the Christmas Foundation Conference bring about an improvement in this kind of thing".

To bring about absolute *openness and transparency* among people working together makes the highest demands of their powers of observation, their goodwill and courage, their tact and ability to express themselves. It can contribute to accelerated development in the process of self-transformation, to reliable *friendliness* between people and to the ability to *engage in true conversation.*

A third transformation sequence emerges:

Communication - openness and transparency - friendliness and the ability to engage in conversation.

The study of the history of the Anthroposophical Society and movement as a process of development can lead to the awakening of a will that is directed towards the forming of a foundation stone for spiritual working together. Working together on an esoteric basis has, at least since the Christmas Foundation Conference, been a central of the Anthroposophical Society and movement. The three qualities described above, which are not yet there, but could emerge from individual self-transformation, may contribute towards the formation of a frm foundation stone for such spiritual co-operation.

- *Taking each other seriously* (authority transformed by implicit trust in each other, and thorough study of spiritual science)

- *Positivity* (criticism transformed by an objective, scientific interest in the faults of one's fellow human beings)

- *Friendliness and the ability to engage in conversation* (communication transformed by unconditional openness and transparency).

References:

[1] Some of what follows has already been published in "Das Goetheanum", 16/2000 and "Gegenwart", 6/1999

[2] Rudolf Steiner, Anthroposophie und Geschichtswissenschaft. Zurich, 7.11.1917, GA 73 (not translated)

[3] Rudolf Steiner, Anthroposophie und Seelenwissenschaft. Zurich, 5.11.1917, GA 73

[4] Eric Hobsbawn, The Age of Extremes, Warner

[5] Yehudi Menuhin, The Beginning of the 90's (p.15)

[6] The Christmas Conference for the Foundation of the General Anthroposophical Society 1923/1924, Anthroposophic Press, 1990. Statutes of the General Anthroposophical Society, Christmas 1923, GA 260a

[7] cf Bodo von Plato, Vom Wiederaufbau zum Dialog. Zur Entwicklung und Kulturwirksamkeit anthroposophischer Arbeit in den vergangenen fünfzig Jahren. In: Der Weg in die Zukunft, Almanach funfzig Jahre, Verlag Frcics Geistesleben. Stuttgart 1997.

[8] Rudolf Steiner, Course for Young Doctors (Mercury Press 1994) Dornach, 6.1.1924, GA 316; see also Rudolf Steiner on the overcoming of anonymous authority in: Psychological distress and the birth pangs of the consciousness soul Zurich, 10.10.1916, GA 168.

[9] Rudolf Steiner, Education for Special Needs: The Curative Education Course, Rudolf Steiner Press 1998. Dornach, 7.7.1924, GA 317

[10] Rudolf Steiner, From Symptom to Reality in Modern History, RSP 1976. Dornach, 25.10.1918, GA 185

[11] The Life, Nature and Cultivation of Anthroposophy RSP 1989. Rudolf Steiner, Letters to Members. Dornach, 10.2.1924, GA260a

Renewing Seed and Human Culture

Bernard Jarman

The practice of biodynamic agriculture leads towards an ever deeper and closer understanding of nature and the hidden alchemy at work within and between her different kingdoms . Our increasing awareness of the interdependence and delicate balance existing between all forms of life in the context of that one global organism that makes up our planet, is awakening a whole new consciousness for life. There is a dawning recognition that each animal and plant species exists, not for itself alone and for its own advancement, but primarily to serve the greater well being of the earth's entire ecosystem.

This radical idea accepted by more and more leading scientists promises to overturn long held theories of evolution and "the struggle for existence." This could have far reaching implications not only for our understanding of nature but also for human social behaviour. Our socio-economic system for so long dominated by competition and the "survival of the fittest" could be transformed through living with the inner picture of service to the common good.

When in 1924 Rudolf Steiner gave the course of lectures on agriculture, which inspired the biodynamic movement, he pointed towards the importance of learning to embrace the whole earth with consciousness and to take account of the influences streaming in from the planets, the fixed stars, and the far reaches of the cosmos. In the seventy five years since these lectures were held, biodynamic agriculture has developed and spread to all parts of the world. Wherever it has taken root new social forms and a renewal of cultural values have been set in train.

Globalisation

Today's global economy and its aggressive exploitation of the earth, places the issue of sustainable agriculture into stark focus. Biodynamic agriculture is consciously sustainable in every detail. As a self-contained evolving organism, every biodynamic farm seeks to rely on its own production to supply the needs of its livestock and on its own compost and manures to provide for the soil's fertility. On the strength of this inner circuit a healthy surplus can provide food for a wide circle of consumers and new relationships of trade and cultural exchange can develop around the farm. In this way a cell for a new social organism begins to emerge.

The current drive to impose biotechnology on a reluctant world threatens to destroy what remains of older sustainable cultures as well as the biodiversity of traditional farming. Until fairly recently every farmer grew and saved his own seed as a matter of course and each had its own uniquely adapted crop variety which differed even from that of his neighbours. Nowadays however, farmers are forced to rely on an increasingly limited range of highly bred, chemical intensive (and if the seed companies have their way - genetically modified) seed varieties, purchased on the global market. Furthermore because hybrid seeds won't breed true, seed saving is rapidly becoming a thing of the past and with disastrous social consequences. As old and tested local plant varieties disappear so too does the independence and self-reliance of the farming community especially in so-called Third World Countries. It can be seen time and time again that a thriving indigenous seed culture reflects a thriving and self-confident people.

Biodynamic Seeds

The development and production of biodynamic seeds has never been so crucial for the future survival of agriculture as it is today. Not only do we need to rescue and save valuable seed varieties from extinction - a vital task in itself - we also need to breed new strong and healthy varieties adapted to biodynamic and organic growing conditions. Much valuable research has already been undertaken during the last decades and individual pioneers have achieved considerable success in using biodynamic methods to improve existing cereal and vegetable varieties as well as to develop new ones. In contrast to modern plant breeding methods in which perceived active genetic constituents of plant varieties are selected and treated in a laboratory, biodynamic seed breeding extends its approach in a holistic way to include the formative influences of the earth, its environment and the world of the stars.

Relationship of Sun and Earth

Fundamental to all life on earth is that primal tension which exists between sun and earth. A tension rooted partly in the gravitational pull between them and partly as a result of the polarity of light and darkness expressed in their essential natures. Plant life expresses itself through endeavouring to weave a bridge between the two and by being at home in darkness and in light by turns.

The sun provides energy, warmth and light with which the plant can build its living substance and unfold its form. Developing step by step through a whole metamorphosis of form it comes to full revelation in the flower. Thereafter it dies back and begins to decay. Generation after generation of plants grow, mature and return to the earth as sustenance for earthworms, micro-organisms and other builders of fertile humus. Each year the seasons are different, warm, wet or cold spells occurring at different moments in the growth cycle causing changes to sap flow, sugar content or checks in development. We may imagine how an impression of the each season lives on as a memory in the living soil. Here in the darkness of the soil, carried in the stream of time, conditions are prepared out of which a new plant can grow.

The sun also draws the plant upward as it grows, leading it towards the utmost periphery of the universe. When the flower opens out growth comes to an end, yet the path upward continues, and as pollen grains it expands out towards the furthest breadths of space. Surrounded by light, warmth and air these minutest of material particles waft through moving air and shimmering starlight until carried by wind or insect they return to create a fertile seed. We may imagine how the whole surrounding cosmos has influenced and is contained within this seed as a result of what has taken place up there among the clouds.

Two different routes are taken to prepare for a new plant's birth - one through the earth and one through the sun. In the living darkness of the soil a place is prepared to receive the seed that has its vitality bequeathed on it by the light filled atmosphere - and by the sun. Planting a seed in the soil is as Goethe recognised the true moment of fertilisation. Only then does the plant have the possibility to grow.

Successful biodynamic plant growing begins with the careful management of soil and compost. Building and maintaining a stable, fertile soil is essential. Organic material of all kinds, from household scraps to garden weeds can be transformed into sweet-smelling compost using the well-tried methods practised throughout the organic movement. The addition to the compost of carefully fermented herb-based biodynamic preparations facilitates a more ordered and thorough transformation in the compost. They also assist the soil on which it is spread to become more sensitive and receptive to the influences streaming in from its environment.

The Preparations

These "biodynamic compost preparations" made from a number of well-known herbs and prepared by a process of enhancement using certain carefully chosen animal organ sheaths, each have a unique quality and specific role to play in the humus-building processes taking place in a compost pile.

· Yarrow (Achillea millefolium). Connected to the potassium and sulphur processes in the soil, the yarrow preparation enables the soil to draw in substances finely distributed in the atmosphere and beyond - which can help to replenish a soil grown tired through many years of cultivation.

· Chamomile (Matricaria Chamomilla). Connected with the calcium process, the chamomile preparation gives the soil a capacity to stabilise its nutrients and to harmonise and invigorate plant growth.

· Stinging Nettle (Urtica dioica). This preparation helps the soil develop an inner sensitivity towards the substances and forces needed by specific plants grown in the soil.

· Oak Bark (Quercus robur). This preparation helps through its connection with calcium to ward off so-called plant diseases and fungus attacks.

· Dandelion (Taraxacum officinale) has a connection to the silica process in plants and is able to activate the influences streaming in from the earth's surrounding.

· Valerian (Valeriana officinalis) is a plant with a strong affinity for warmth and order. It gives the plant a warmth blanket and stimulates the activity of phosphorus.

When placed as a group yet individually sited into a compost heap, the effects of these preparations slowly radiate out through the compost thence to the soil.

Two further preparations are applied directly on the soil and to the plant. The formative forces of plant development can be enhanced with these "horn manure" and "horn silica" preparations. These are special field sprays made from cow manure and ground quartz which have undergone a process of fermentation in a cow horn beneath the soil during winter and summer respectively.

Horn manure sprayed on the soil helps draw the plant roots down into a healthy connection with the earth while horn silica sprayed directly onto the growing plant at critical moments in its development helps to regulate and vitalise the plants fluid metabolism, increase sugar content, its general quality and enhance the vitality of seeds.

These specifically biodynamic measures taken together with sound organic practice serve to create a vital and well-balanced soil in which the seeds of chosen plant varieties can find optimum germination and growing conditions.

Sowing Times

Not only is the relationship between sun and earth important. When seeds of high quality are sought the subtle influences streaming in from the twelve constellations of the zodiac also need considering.

In their daily and yearly movement across the sky (as perceived from our perspective), the stars are in a constantly changing relationship to the earth. Within the short space of 24 hours, the entire sphere of the stars passes across the sky. Each day and night the sun, moon and all the stars make this journey. Less immediately apparent are the movements in the reverse direction - of the wandering stars, the planets and the moon. Moving across the sky at different rates, they create a wonderfully complex network of relationships with one another, with the earth and against the background of the fixed stars in the zodiac. How their movements influence life on the earth forms the basis for the well-known "Biodynamic Sowing and Planting Calendar" produced by Maria Thun.

It is with the ever-changing position of the moon as it moves form west to east through each constellation of the zodiac in turn that this calendar is primarily concerned. During the course of four weeks the moon will have passed through all twelve constellations. This cycle or rhythm of the moon is not to be confused with the more well known waxing and waning cycle which has to do with the relationship of the moon to the sun.

Research undertaken by Maria Thun over several decades shows how the moon's position in the zodiac can effect plant growth. The unique formative influences pouring down on the earth from the twelve constellations are strengthened each in turn as the moon passes before.

As recognised in the wisdom of astrology, the constellations are linked to the four elements - earth, water, air and fire, which in turn have a connection to the four parts of the plant - root, leaf, flower and fruit. By growing aware of the moon's position, the gardener can choose to plant carrots on a root day i.e. when the moon stands before an earth constellation, or cabbages on a leaf day.

The enhancement possible through working with awareness for stellar influences is especially important when seeking to improve on and develop seed varieties.

Diversity of growing conditions

Plants grown under different soil and climatic conditions will follow different growth patterns and the qualities in the crop will vary correspondingly.

Consider how different it must be for say a beetroot growing on an island buffeted by the salt spray and winds of the ocean as compared with one growing in a lush and protected walled garden in Southern England; or again of potatoes growing on the flood plains of the river Severn compared to those growing on thin soils in the bracing climate of a Scottish hillside.

Biodynamic plant breeders make use of these differences in soil and climate to stretch, broaden and increase the vigour of these varieties. It is a complex and demanding field of work requiring close attention to the smallest detail while being aware of the widest connections and influences at work on the earth as a whole.

Rigorous scientific enquiry and an ability to distinguish essential from the non-essential is crucial while at the same time an art of observation must be learnt, born of daily and yearly husbandry practice. Only the farmer will know whether the crop of wheat is healthy and where it can be improved. A trained eye is then needed to see which ears of corn hold the best potential and to know which grains shall be kept for future use.

In days gone by seed growing was an integral part of the farming year, it also formed a focus for rural community life. Today this has gone and it is our task once again to bring the seeds of our food plants to the forefront of our consciousness. The production of biodynamic seeds is clearly a responsibility of biodynamic farmers everywhere. They cannot carry it alone however. Wherever seeds are grown, opportunities exist for the involvement of a wider community and for their help with the work of selection, weeding, harvesting and cleaning. Unlike the produce which is grown to be consumed, seeds are there to enable the farm to exist on into the future.

The Biodynamic Agricultural Association is promoting the development of biodynamic seeds as one of its core tasks and has recently set up a seed fund. More information on this and other aspects of biodynamic agriculture is available from:

The Biodynamic Agricultural Association,
Painswick Inn Project, Gloucester Street, Stroud, Glos, GL5 1QG
Tel / Fax: 01453 759501
Email: bdaa@biodynamic.freeserve.co.uk

Anthroposophy and Psychiatry[1]

Dr. James Dyson

The Mind/Body Problem

If we go back to the early 1920s, when Steiner was beginning to develop his medical work, medicine at that time stood very much at a crossroads. A few years after Steiner gave his medical lectures, insulin and vitamin B12 were discovered. Shortly after that, in the early 1930s, the sulphonamides were developed, then followed antibiotics during the second World War, and in the 1950s there followed the main impact on psychiatric medication, which has transformed the management of a great deal of mental illness. I am referring particularly to the major tranquillisers, the anticonvulsive drugs, the antidepressants, and so on. It is amazing to think that at the time when Rudolf Steiner was speaking, manipulation of the bodily basis of much that we would now call mental functioning had not even started; and yet at that time psychoanalysis had already made a beginning.

Freud's work was to some degree becoming established and it wasn't going to be long before the work of Carl Jung also came into the foreground. Steiner had major reservations about psychoanalysis, but it is important for us to fully understand just what these were based on. He did not, for instance, deny the validity of the concept of the unconscious. He stressed, however, that without an understanding of the spiritual nature of the human being, including reincarnation and karma, and without an understanding of how substances in the body really support the life of soul, any attempt to penetrate into the sphere of the so-called "unconscious" or "sub-conscious" would be fraught with misunderstanding. He stressed, moreover, that any attempt to penetrate this realm would involve, at the very least, an awareness of the threshold between what belongs essentially to the soul-spiritual nature of the human being as it has evolved over many incarnations and the everyday conscious experience of the self. This corresponds to the threshold between

[1] Based on the opening lecture given by Dr. James Dyson at a conference on Mental Health held at Triform Community, Hudson, New York on 29th February 1996 corrected and, in parts, slightly elaborated by the lecturer. Shortly to be included in a new series in the U.S.

the point-centred consciousness of our earthly waking ego and the peripheral consciousness of our life of will. Although an awareness of the existence of an "unconscious" had surfaced during the early part of this century, its interpretation without a basis in spiritual scientific training and understanding was, in Steiner's view, at best misleading and at worst dangerous. He was particularly concerned with some of the more specifically sexual interpretations which dominated Freudian methods at the beginning and which, in his view, had already created many illusory interpretatios.

Steiner gave a particular indication with respect to our understanding of mental illness, which redresses the one-sidedness of the psychoanalytical approach. He emphasized that one must first understand the bodily basis of the soul life before trying to interpret what comes to expression in the soul as such. Alongside this statement he suggested that with respect to the nature of organic physical illness, one should search for its origin more in the realm of the soul and spirit.

You can see how he was, in a way, both anticipating and countering a trend that was to increase in its momentum during the following decades, a trend which, to this day, dominates current thinking as strongly as ever. I am referring to the trend to separate our understanding of the human being into a biochemical model on the one hand, and a psychotherapeutic, psychoanalytic model on the other, the former without reference to the soul and spirit, the latter without reference to the actual bodily basis of consciousness. It might seem that Steiner was anticipating the biological basis of psychiatry in pointing to bodily dysfunction as underlying much mental illness. He was, however, speaking from a very different perspective from that which has since evolved and which has given rise to the current "psychopharmaca". He was challenging us to see physiological processes and substance transformations within the body as the basis or the expression of the soul-spiritual element, while at the same time to see soul-spiritual processes as being accompanied on some level by physiological ones. I would say that the central challenge of the anthroposophical contribution to psychiatry lies just in this - to bring together the realm of creative spirit with an understanding substance and metabolism.

The Two Streams of Time

This is a challenge which has by no means, as yet, fulfilled its full potential although very encouraging and exciting beginnings have certainly already been made. Behind this there lies the deeper challenge of understanding the nature of matter or substance altogether in its soul-spiritual aspect. This is of course the general challenge of anthroposophical medicine. The part which belongs specifically to psychiatry is to see how the substances and processes which these substances undergo in the organs are connected to possible deviations or aberrations of consciousness, which psychiatry describes and attempts to address.

I would now like to take a big step and mention something else which will not at first seem to be directly connected to this theme, namely, Steiner's description of two streams of time. The one which we are aware of in our everyday consciousness goes from the present into the future. There is, however, another stream which works in the opposite direction and which comes from the future into the present! These two streams of time, the former connected more to the conscious astral body, the latter more to the etheric, meet within the human being. They meet in the realm of the ego, which is the only instrument of consciousness that can really integrate past and future, thereby bringing the destiny that we bring with us from former incarnations into the freedom-space from which new impulses may be born.

Much mental and soul confusion arises in the encounter between these two streams of time, even some forms of mental illness may arise from this. The substance-processes taking place in our organs, contain within them the seeds for our future consciousness. If these seeds are released prematurely from their etheric basis in the organic life, and enter consciousness too soon, they will produce delusion, deception, hallucination, fear, anxiety, mania. All possible forms of soul aberrations may come about through the tendency for the etheric forces within the organs to rush forward into the future too soon. On the other hand, when the forces working from the past bind us too strongly to our organs, then tendencies to hardening and sclerosis take hold of the body. We become locked into our earthly personalities and thereby lies the basis for the more characteristic physical illnesses. In the healthy human being, the latter processes predominate in waking life, and the former during sleep. During waking life the etheric up-building processes in our organs become subordinate to the more conscious experiences of soul life - and vice versa. The two streams of time also oscillate between our waking experience and our sleeping - hence the possibility for, amongst other things, dreams with prophetic overtones to come about.

Most of us will know that Waldorf education emphasizes the fact that the organic forces that build the body during the first seven years, and which also belong more to the state of sleep, become released to some extent at the age of seven. In fact, they only become released from the head and nerve-sense organisation, where they become available after this time for thinking and memory. The etheric substance which has formed and shaped this part of our body is the same substance through which, at a later stage of development, we are able to think. We must imagine that this is only the first of many etheric metamorphoses that may take place during the course of life. The etheric forces that release themselves for thinking belong essentially to the instrument of the brain. By the time we are seven, the brain, which is an organ whose development proceeds much faster than any other organ, has reached a certain completion. We call this stage neurological maturity, which is witnessed, for example, in the establishment of dominance and in nerve myalination in the central nervous system through which the basic pathways of sensory integration are laid down. We also know that the actual nerve cells in the brain, even from before the time we were born, have been slowly dying and degenerating. In fact, degenerative processes accompany our brain and nerve sense system during the course of our life. This is the corollary of the fact that our brain and nerve-sense system form, for the most part, the basis of waking day consciousness.

The Polarities of Brain and Spleen, Image Memory and Substance Memory:

This "slow death" of the physical body in the brain is that which allows the etheric forces which formed and sculptured it and which contributed to its organic development, to be used for conscious thinking activity. With the other organs, however, this process does not take place to anything like the same extent. If we consider an organ which stands in a certain polarity to the brain, namely the spleen, then we find an organ which hardly appears to be a physical organ at all. In contrast to the brain it lacks internal form and structure. Also, unlike the brain, it is an organ which is continually regenerating itself. If we consider the spleen, however, we have an organ which carries within itself the basis not of our self-conscious image memory, but of our substance memory. In the modern world we call substance memory the science of immunology. The importance of our physiological uniqueness in the form of our immunological memory, has become, in recent years, almost general knowledge. Without it we are unable to maintain our identity against the outside world. The spleen can be removed without apparent detriment to health, although, in a child, its loss leaves some degree of compromised immunity, depending amongst other things on the age when this happens. It is an organ with a kind of peripheral sphere of activity. I am referring to the millions of smaller lymph nodes throughout the body which have a kind of satellite function in relation to the spleen itself, but which can exist independently after the foundations of immunity have been acquired.

We are dependent not only on our image memory for an earthly biography, but on our substance memory too, although it is not so immediately obvious why this should be the case. Animals, for example, do not have individually based immunological specificity. Immunological identity belongs more to the species. Animals, however, do not have individual biographies. The animal's identity is "species-based", not "specimen-based". In recent years, the immune system has become threatened as never before. Indeed, it is no longer something which can be just taken for granted.

Without our brain we would not know who we were when we woke up in the morning - and without this possibility earthly consciousness would be chaotic, as indeed it becomes in certain conditions of cerebral degeneration. If image memory is connected with the brain, and substance memory with the spleen and immune system, must it not follow from this that our image memory is the basis of our waking-day consciousness of self, and our substance memory, the basis of our sleeping or unconscious self? This may be identified with our true individuality or higher-self working and weaving between incarnations.

From this perspective it is perhaps possible to make the connection between individual human immunity and personal karma although I am aware that at first hearing this may appear to be a big jump to make. Our normal habits of thought would lead us to assume that metabolism proceeds in its own way and that we meet our karma from a completely different realm, in a somewhat metaphysical manner. I strongly suspect, however, that this is another trick of dualistic thinking. We meet the outside world, essentially in three ways:- through the portal of the senses, the portal of the breath and the portal of metabolism. In all three areas, substance is in fact involved; in the metabolism the connection is very obvious, in the breath we meet substance of air and through the senses we meet light. Just as in our metabolism we have first to break down and digest what we eat before it is rebuilt, a similar process must also take place in our senses. Our entire nerve-sense organisation has the characteristic that it first has to hold back sense impressions and digest them, as it were, before they can become integrated and internalised in the life of soul. The processes of sensory digestion and substance digestion are working together all the time, continually playing into one another. It is quite clear that we meet our destiny and karma from that which we encounter via our senses. What we have breathed in and digested through our senses unites itself inwardly with that stream of substance which has first been broken down in our digestive organs. In this way individual destiny becomes imprinted within the very substance of our bodies. Can you sense how the normal boundaries of logic, which separate substance from spirit, begin to disappear! The dualistic distinction between these two realms is not quite so clear any more. Ahrimanic forces have, of course, taken hold of the material realm, and are continually trying to widen the gap between their realm and the realm of creative spiritual being. On the other hand, however, the substances which we eat have been created by photosynthesis from the light. The substances of earth and light essentially belong together, although these two concepts have become mutually estranged.

During the time of our embryonic development and, to a lesser extent, throughout our childhood, the substance-building processes of our body are at their most creative. The child's unconscious life of will is working with those very etheric forces which will later develop into forces of consciousness. At the beginning of life these forces are involved in the forming of the sense organs themselves, which become built and inter-connected like resonance chambers, through which what is received from the outside world can take shape within bodily substance. The etheric processes whereby this happens have been called by Steiner the life processes. Let me outline on the board the form of an eye, with a lens and so forth, as the most obvious example of a sense organ. We can immediately identify that an interaction is taking place, mediated by the eye, between that which comes towards it from the outside world in the form of outer light and that which we bring towards the perception from inner experience. In theory we can imagine that we first experience the light as a pure sense perception or percept. However, for a human being a pure percept can scarcely exist. The moment the outer world impinges upon any sense organ, it is taken up and "digested" by inner processes working on a more or less unconscious level. Contrary to theories of ordinary sensory psychology, which attribute everything of a cognitive nature to the nerves, these are connected to processes in the blood which carries the element of will. Through this digestion of the percept in its encounter with blood-processes there arises an entire spectrum of possibilities of soul life. Broadly speaking, the life element of the blood brings the instinct and drive towards the percept, and between these two poles there arises everything connected with concept, memory, feeling and judgement. The precise order in which these may be arranged needn't concern us just now. The formation of a concept in relation to a percept, already involves a degree of judgement. Within this backdrop we can see that the seven life- processes actively transform what to begin with came towards us as a purely outer phenomenon into something internalised and incorporated into the sphere of soul and body. This process which, as I said, is most active in the developmental period of embryonic life and childhood is, of course, liable to all manner of aberrations. Just bring to mind for a moment something like sensory deprivation on the one hand, or overstimulation on the other. One can then go on to imagine how, if a child meets inconsistent behaviour, or even frank abuse, the judgement-forming processes of the soul will be impaired. The earlier this takes place, the more deeply rooted will be the aberrant forms and structural developments in the body arising from it.

The bodily basis for the future life of soul depends intimately on how the life-processes interact with the sense organs, particularly during the developmental stage. It is also through this process that the adult relationship between the etheric and the astral bodies is slowly established in the organs. In fact, the character of this relationship is distinct for each organ - and organs are just as much sense organs as they are metabolic ones. In this way the developmental basis is established for much that later on expresses itself in the form of psychiatric illness.

The Seven Life Processes and the Main Internal Organs

I will have to assume for the moment that what Steiner has described about the seven life-processes is not entirely unfamiliar to you. They are connected, of course, to the seven planets, which Steiner has also described as having a connection to the seven main internal organs. During the course of embryonic and child development, the astral forces, which belong to the planetary realm, and the etheric forces work very closely together. Through the particular affinity between the organ and the planet, a kind of resonance chamber arises in the body for each of the seven planetary spheres which, when taken together, comprise the entire astral body. The moon sphere, which is most closely connected with the earth, forms the brain. The Saturn sphere, which is the most removed from the earth, forms the spleen. The Jupiter sphere and the Mars sphere work together in the formation of liver and gall bladder. Mercury works into the lung and Venus into the kidney. The planetary forces working within each organ help the etheric forces of the organ to remain held and integrated in the body. They bring boundaries to bear on the otherwise expansive tendencies of the etheric body. During the developmental period, the relationship between the etheric body and the astral body is laid down in the organs themselves. Astral forces have more of an affinity to connect with the sense impressions from the outside world, in relation to which they then unfold as faculties of soul. As I have said, each organ is in fact just as much a sense organ as it is a metabolic organ. In the brain we see an organ whose substance comes closest to death - thereby it is particularly suited to forming the basis of waking consciousness. In the spleen we see the opposite processes at work. Here the blood processes, which belong to the very depths of our unconscious life of will, have taken hold of everything coming from the outside world and metamorphosed it into bodily substance.

Brain and Spleen

In the brain, the forces of the outer world, i.e., the sense impressions, become dominant and the astral body and the etheric body both withdraw from the physical body after creating their most complex imprint within it. This may be seen in the language of modern brain physiology in terms of the complex network of nerve growth factors, which are activated only to the extent that the child's life of will is aroused to a creative relationship to sense perceptions. Perhaps we are seeing in these processes what Steiner has described in referring to a co-operation between blood and nerve processes. After the imprint has been created they become emancipated from the body, thereby becoming free for the conscious life of soul. In the brain the outer world is always in danger of conquering the inner world; that is to say, through the brain we lose touch with our inner being.

In the spleen, however, we can say the opposite, namely that the inner forces of self are continually triumphing over the forces of the outer world. The astral and etheric bodies remain active metabolically in the blood processes and the spleen therefore retains a strong connection to the unconscious ego which remains active in the body directly rather than via the kind of structural imprint which is to be found in the brain. We may therefore say that the way the life processes take hold of these two organs expresses a polarity.

Lung and Liver

Between the spleen and the brain we find the inner organs of the liver and the lung. In the lung we see an organ which is, in many ways, similar to the brain. It has a very strong and hard endoskeleton in the form of its bronchial tree, composed of cartilaginous rings.   Steiner has characterised the lung as having the closest relationship of all the organs to earthly thoughts - that is to say, to the brain. Steiner connects the lung, for instance, to the ability to memorise facts and figures, quantity rather than quality, for example, telephone directory memories. He describes all our memories as being imprinted into the etheric sheath or etheric surface of our organs - and the actual etheric forces through which the lung has been formed have a particular affinity to earthly thoughts, to everything that lends itself to being weighed, measured and quantified. Steiner has called this aspect of our etheric body, the life ether. These life ether forces which work on a bodily level in a kind of additive way, as is expressed, for example, in the continuous growth pattern of a fungus, these life ether forces in the lung become something like the guardians of those sense perceptions which belong to the essentially earthly element of cognition based on factual memory.

We are all very familiar with various clinical ways in which this comes to expression. For the curative teacher, for example, the child will come to mind who can sometimes quite literally remember every single detail of everything that has happened, not only today and the day before, but perhaps last week, last month, last year, or even ten years ago. Some children display remarkable encyclopaedic memories of this kind.

We see a similar phenomenon, albeit in a different form, in the adult who displays obsessive tendencies or fixed ideas. In a fixed idea a spiritual happening becomes de-contextualised - it is made into something of an isolated entity. The way the ether body works in the lung is continually appealing to this kind of isolating, fixating tendency. The forces of the outer world are therefore not being so thoroughly internalised, digested and metamorphosed into phantasy as they are in other organs, for instance, the liver. The outer world imposes itself on the soul in too direct a form - hence we can say that in the lung, as in the brain, the outer forces are, relatively speaking, conquering the inner forces.

Just as the lung stands in an intimate relation to the brain and the nerve-sense system, in so far as it isolates the individual elements from the whole being, making a kind of self-contained entity from them, so the liver, in contrast, is an organ which cooperates very closely with the spleen in the whole system of metabolism. Just as the sense organs all converge on the brain, where the sense impressions become metabolised within the life of soul, so does the intestinal tract converge in the liver, through which substances from the outside world begin to be elaborated into the unique substances of our own bodies.

This substance-building activity of the liver, when imbued with the impulses from the spleen, also forms the bodily basis of our will life, but it exerts its influence a little closer to the level of the soul than does the spleen. If the spleen is the guardian of our pre-earthly intentions, then the liver is already attempting to bring these to manifestation here and now on this side of the threshold. It is the organ which gives the bodily basis for the exercising of initiative and motivation, it is the origin of our vitality and, to some extent also, our enthusiasm. All these soul functions are intimately connected with the way metabolic processes interface with what is taken in from our senses. It is possible, indeed up to a point normal, for cognitive life, which has developed itself on the basis of our sense perceptions, to follow a different direction to the life of deeper motivation or intentionality. Without the tension that arises between these two realms, both connected as they are to our life of will, but in very different ways, we would not find the power to pursue our earthly biography from a condition of inner freedom. However, it is possible for the normal healthy tension that should exist between these two realms to diverge to such a degree that the seeds are planted for a real split between the cognitive world and the world of more unconscious will life. This may manifest itself fairly quickly in some form of depression or inability to put intention into deed, or be delayed by years, decades or even life-times! Liver physiology is in turn connected with the biliary system. Secretory processes of the liver are focused in the production of bile, which is stored in the gall bladder before being ejected into the intestines. Here it encounters substances from the outside world and contributes to their breakdown. Biliary processes are even more strongly connected to the more conscious pole of will than is the liver. The liver stands at a kind of mid point between the biliary processes, through which our will encounters the outside world, and the spleen, which is the guardian of the deeper nature of the will. Any obstruction or congestion in the process of bile production or excretion may have a laming effect on the conscious life of the will and this may be often observed in medical and psychiatric practice if one is awake to this possibility.

The liver is an organ with a strong kinship to the fluid realm. If the substances of the outer world overwhelm the liver, then it becomes something like a stagnant pool of water. Substances are taken in, but are not vitalised and may sit there heavily, as it were undigested or unpenetrated. When substances are incompletely digested, allergies may arise. Classical allergies are fairly easy to identify but nowadays one meets an increasing number of a more insidious variety which may manifest only through more subtle symptoms such as tiredness after eating, loss of vitality and so on. This tendency is often exacerbated in a clinical depression, or in someone with chronic fatigue syndrome, where a vicious circle of interactions is often seen.

You may remember the very famous example from Steiner's Curative Education Course of the child who has difficulty with his will in actually stepping into a tram. Steiner connects this description of a child who is, as it were, paralysed in his will, who is unable to release himself from the conscious life of thought into the spontaneity of a deed, to a weakness in the activity of the liver. He actually suggests that the disorder may have been inherited. Whenever weakness of will manifests itself in the child or adult in any form, we can ask ourselves if the liver - or for that matter the gall bladder - is in need of support. This sometimes shows itself at times of transition in life, for instance, in the menopause or following a pregnancy. At both these transition-times a person is increasingly vulnerable to suffering from depression. During the menopause, a further metamorphosis of organic etheric forces into the conscious soul life is taking place - or at least the potential is there for this to happen. Forces which have been active on a bodily level in the glands until this time become available for new soul-spiritual activity or development. If they are not appropriately taken up, however, congestion of the liver and biliary system may ensue. Indeed, moderate degrees of this are almost normal at such times, since processes of metamorphosis are usually only gradually accomplished.

On a more day by day level, we also experience physiological transitions at three o'clock in the morning and three o'clock in the afternoon. At three o'clock in the afternoon, blood sugar levels are usually on the low side, signifying that the substance building aspect of liver function is at its weakest at this time. At three o'clock in the morning, however, bile production is at its weakest point. Both these times of transition tend to be difficult periods during the day or night for people struggling with depressive illnesses. Waking at three o'clock in the morning with morbid thoughts - that is to say, thoughts which it is not possible to properly digest and integrate into the waking consciousness, are very familiar examples of this. In more severe forms of manic depressive illness, tendencies of this kind can be much more dramatic.

The Liver and Altered States of Mind

Steiner has connected the liver with that part of the etheric body which is called the chemical ether. This is also sometimes called the tone ether, the number ether or the sound ether. Through this ether, physical growth is inwardly organised according to the inner harmonies of number and measure, which also become manifest in the inner harmonies of music. When this etheric quality becomes prematurely released into the realm of soul, the stream of time coming from the future to the present is likely to overwhelm the normal state of waking consciousness. All manner of experiences can then arise to which the soul feels connected but no longer in a free way. Such things as ideas of reference, déja vu phenomena, and even deeper states of paranoia, may thereby arise. The etheric forces which are particularly connected with the liver give us the experience of becoming contextualised in our environment. When these forces unfold their activity too strongly in consciousness, a disturbance in our relationship to the surrounding environment may ensue. Paranoia is one of the most frequent forms that such a disturbance takes. One feels threatened by the environment, but in a very personalised way, almost as though the substances of the outside world are working their own life out at our own expense! Paranoia may, in turn, be a fairly transient phenomenon, with a more neurotic character, or it may be major symptom of a severe psychotic depression, or even a schizophrenic illness.

I mentioned a few moments ago that an astral quality from one or other of the planetary spheres works together with the etheric body of a particular organ, constraining these forces and guarding against their tendency to jump, as it were, too quickly out of the body, too quickly into the future. Whenever that planetary or astral activity within an organ becomes weakened - and weaknesses may be inherent or acquired - the soul becomes vulnerable to encountering forces from the etheric body which it should not meet until after death or until one is suitably prepared for a conscious encounter with the spiritual world. Any drug or poison will also to some degree deflect the life-processes from their bodily manifestation, leading to the premature release of etheric forces into the soul realm. This phenomenon forms the basis for the anthroposophical understanding of certain aspects of drug abuse. Different drugs may display certain organ affinities - for instance, the qualitative effects of cocaine may be seen in terms of the lung, of LSD more in terms of the kidney. What one is then meeting as a disturbance of the etheric forces of the organs is also a disturbance on the life-processes of the organs. It is a kind of foretaste of the experience that we meet after death, when we see the panorama of the life that we have just lived. After death this experience - known as the etheric tableau experience - normally only happens when our entire ether body becomes freed from our physical body. At the time of our death this experience is strongly held within the sphere of the Being of Christ and the Spirit of the Guardian of the Threshold. If this happens prematurely, albeit only in a modified form through a drug, the soul may experience later difficulties or impediments in returning properly into the body and this may also sow the seed for different forms of disorientation and dislocation of the conscious life of will. I cannot expand in this talk on the theme of drug abuse or addiction. I would, however, like to point to the close connection that has often been noted between certain drug experiences and certain spiritual experiences. This becomes much more readily comprehensible when we are able to understand it in terms of the organs. The forces that are released from the etheric activities of the organs, the forces more bound up with the inner side of the life processes, are expressions of the living activity of spiritual beings that are still active within the substance of our own body. The threshold to the substance-building processes is indeed the same as the threshold to the spiritual world altogether. We meet the spiritual world where the substance-building processes of our bodily organs are taking place. But it is quite a different thing to meet this through a process of inner training and inner development, or to meet it after death when these forces have been naturally released, so to speak, than it is to do so through substance abuse or through weaknesses within the activity of the planetary sphere belonging to a particular organ. For the anthroposophical doctor and psychiatrist, the field of possible medicinal therapy opens up at this point through, for example, an understanding of the connections between the different metals, the planets and the organs. It is not possible to develop this further, however, at this point.

Child Development

I hope that this broad overview serves to indicate how anthroposophy spans so many aspects of the realm of psychiatry, opening up new possibilities of understanding, of diagnosis and also of therapy. I have also tried to point out the extent to which the realm of psychiatry and the realm of inner development or initiation are intimately connected. I have often had the feeling that much that is met in the realm of psychiatry may be a kind of result or expression of an incompleted process of initiation in a former life. I would certainly not suggest that this is so in every case, but an insufficiently prepared initiation may be the result of an attempt to cross the threshold into the spiritual world too soon. We see the same gesture becoming manifest when our etheric body in the one or other of our organs wishes to become released too quickly. Thoughts such as this are sometimes helpful in those cases of mental illness in which it is not possible to discern their origin in this life on earth, and with which a person may have to live for a whole incarnation.

It is, however, often possible to understand a great deal of mental illness or psychological disturbance in relation to childhood development. Nowadays childhood development is under threat and it is very difficult for most people to go through childhood in such a way that they achieve a healthy soul-spiritual penetration of the body. Many things are responsible for this, including poor nutrition, an education that has no respect for phases of bodily development and which already draws organic processes too soon from the body into the realm of soul; through a general deprivation of what Steiner has called the bodily senses - that is to say, the senses of touch, life, movement and balance. When the life- processes withdraw from these senses too quickly, the astral body is not able to create a sufficiently strong resonance chamber or imprint for itself within the physical and etheric bodies. This may show itself in later life in the form of soul insecurities, anxieties, hyperactivity and so on. Childhood is also threatened through the general dissolution of society. Conventional securities, accepted modes of behaviour, and so on, are rightly falling to one side, but all too often parents are not able to replace them from their own individual resources. We continually find ourselves thrown back upon ourselves, needing to rely on personal judgements too soon before the organic basis of our body has been properly equipped to fulfil this task. This crumbling of the social and moral fabric of society throws the developing child all too easily into a state of turmoil. At an increasingly early age the adolescent has often to encounter the sense of inner void, meaninglessness, the realm of inner darkness. Existential questions to do with self-identity confront the adolescent nowadays almost as a normal phenomenon, whereas even 30 years ago the securities that applied to generation after generation acted as a form of protection against this.

When we really meet the existential question, "Who am I?", the answer never can be found in the outside world which we meet via our senses. It can only be found from that same eternal self which lives behind the threshold of our physical organs. Between our conscious experience of self and our eternal being, however, there lies that interface of soul which I mentioned a few minutes ago - the realm in which there is an ongoing battle between our conscious self and our eternal self. The bodily basis of our life often looks for ease, comfort and security. Spiritual intentions on the other hand threaten earthly securities, and deepseated fears, doubts and so on may be evoked by them in the soul. These forces belong to those instincts and, to some degree necessary, egoistic drives which are implanted within our physical body and which work into our earthly personality at a deeply unconscious level. These forces are constantly enticing us to build our identity on the outside world - on something upon which we can apparently rely and from which we can derive a certain sense of security and predictability. Everything that derives from the outside world and which we meet through our senses - particularly those aspects to which the lung has an affinity, such as obsessions, fixed ideas and so on - all these will tend to offer us apparent solutions in the face of the spiritual challenge in meeting the inner void.

In so many of the psychiatric illnesses of adolescence, we see particularly clearly how this phenomenon comes to expression prematurely. I refer, for instance, to the phenomenon of eating disorders, which have almost become a kind of epidemic at the present time.

Multiple Personality Disorders

In more recent years psychiatry has developed a new interest in the personality, particularly through descriptions of so-called multiple personality disorders - now referred to as dissociative identity disorders. In this type of condition the tension between opposing elements is no longer held or integrated within the framework of the single person, but different elements become seeds around which apparently independent personalities develop. There is sometimes a lack of continuity of ego consciousness and even memory between the one personality and the other - a fragmentation has taken place. The more severe forms of this disturbance are usually connected with sexual abuse during early life. I am sure that through deepening our understanding of the co-operation of the senses and life processes during the time of childhood development, our insights into this type of disturbance would take on new dimensions. In fact, a number of anthroposophical psychiatrists have already begun to do just this.

As many of us are aware, however, this phenomenon can lead to some of the most frightening of phenomena which we as human beings may have to encounter. When an ego fragmentation takes place, islands of our etheric and astral bodies have become dislocated from the overall sphere of the ego organisation. It is here that the borderline between the realm of medicine and psychiatry on the one hand and that of social and personal morality, becomes almost indistinguishable. Those of you who are familiar with the works of Scott Peck, particularly his book "People of the Lie", will be aware that he addresses this problem. He challenges contemporary psychiatry to build a new scientific understanding of the realm of evil, stressing how until the present time this realm has been considered to fall outside the scope of science. This book was not written with dissociative identity disorders particularly in mind, but I am sure that there is a close connection between these phenomena and many of his descriptions. He relates much of what he has to say to possession - a concept which, until recently, was considered to be virtually medieval. I think that this book by Scott Peck is courageous and in some ways quite masterly. However, it exemplifies the difficulty that modern psychiatry finds itself in when it attempts to confront the spiritual nature of the human being without any points of spiritual reference, or any way of connecting the realm of substance to the realm of spirit. With only vague generalisations regarding the unconscious to draw upon, it inevitably encounters a dichtomy which is fundamentally unresolvable.

As I began my talk by saying, I think that it is just this potential that is unique to the anthroposophical contribution to psychiatry. The original polarity between substance and creative spirit arose during the time of the Fall on Old Lemuria. From this time onwards the creative world of the spirit and the actual substantial happenings in matter started to separate. We are now at the point in human evolution when out of their own nature these two forces will continue to diverge ever more and more strongly. Steiner forecast that by the end of the 20th century we would be blighted by epidemics of mental illness of one kind or another - and I am sure that, amongst other things, eating disorders and dissociative disorders are foremost among the examples that could be cited to bear out his prediction. I believe that ultimately the task of mental illness is to stimulate in us the call to inner development, to truly know ourselves. Whereas up until the present time we had a certain licence to decide not to follow this path, it is nowadays almost imperative to do so if we are to confront and deal with problems, if not exactly in epidemic, then certainly in escalating proportions. Modes of being that were once regarded as unusual pathologies become ever more and more accepted as part of normal development. Unless a sufficiently strong impulse is ignited in humankind to hear the call of anthroposophy, then this separation between substance and spirit will continue. It will then become increasingly difficult for human bodies to sustain a basis for integrated ego consciousness into the future. They then become the basis for the activity of those evil beings - so called "anti-spirits" of personality to which Steiner has given the name of "Asuras". The loss of immunological identity that we are also witnessing at the present time is, I believe, the mirror image of this. That is to say, it is the polar expression of the same phenomenon. In the realm of psychiatry, the possibility of the conscious ego to integrate itself with its own karma is threatened, and at the level of immunology, the possibility for the unconscious organisation of the ego to penetrate physical substance is also threatened. We live in a time when developments are accelerating around us, but this was something that Rudolf Steiner anticipated at the beginning of this century and which anthroposophy is intended to help us to master. We are, however, still only at the beginning of doing just this - it lies in the hands of each of us to help to realise this aim.

Ready! Aye, Ready!

Alex Naylor

The single greatest challenge granted to those striving to present the anthroposophical world conception is: How can we portray a picture of man as a spiritual being living in a material form which, can counteract on the one side that of man as intelligent animal, and on the other, man as organic machine? It is this *battle* - now let's not beat about the bush here - for it is a battle for the vision of man, in a long war, that is our peculiar responsibility. As far as the scope of this article will permit, I will endeavour to provide a glimpse into how this challenge is taking on a specific form.

For many years now I have been lecturing to both undergraduate and post-graduate students in mythology, theology and philosophy, attempting to show that the two Greek words *mythos* and *logos* have divine origin and like the other small words *I, love* and *wisdom*, mythology is utterly not understood, neither in its essence nor its application. *Mythos* meaning *story* or *account, Logos* meaning *word/god*, in the sense of Heraclitus or more familiarly so, in that of St. John the Divine. In the shell of a nut, mythologos - mythology - the Story of God, the Account of God - the Word of God - all are synonymous, and since Christ says, (St. John 10 v.34) "...Is it not written in your law, I said, Ye are Gods?..." there remains the issue of how to counter the following, both in ourselves and in others. That we live in an era which has already long since abolished man as a living spirit need not deter us, nor that we are now not far removed from abolishing him as a soul. For it places us precisely on that part of the front to which we which earlier alluded.

The task firstly is to eliminate unnecessary obstacles in the way of a clear view of our primary objective. Unnecessary obstacles are preconceived notions possessed by those of 'everyday mind' - by no means only those of scientific mind - who pride themselves on accepting only that which is directly understood by the concept of 'proof' resulting from sensory observation, the thinking applied to it and the concepts resulting from it.

The Apple

In the scientific community a theorem is accepted as proven when the scientist lays down specific conditions, the duplication of which, if faithfully undertaken by any individual, in both form and order, will lead to the same manifestation of result no matter how often this is repeated. It is thereby "proven". To this end, one can use the humble apple as an example (how often the apple features in myth, history and science!) in leading our fellows from the sense perceptible to the non perceptible in an effort to retain an open mind. In this I have found the apple a 'very useful piece of kit'. Holding the apple, one asks an audience to assume they are perceiving something of which they have no experience. How are they going to understand it? To form a concept uniting percept with object as a thinking subject? This often presents a challenge. Initially they cannot call it an apple, or a fruit, anything. It can only be identified through thinking applied to the visual percept, for example: red, round, etc. One slices the apple in half, giving a half to one person showing the other to the remainder. The recipient then already has a whole new world of experience lacking for the others, through touch. Shown that it is safe to eat, the lecturer having led by example, the holder feels safe to consume a chunk of the unknown object. What do we have here? Remaining entirely within the realm of the five accepted senses, the audience still only has experience of the apple through the sense of sight and probably hearing, and the thinking they can apply to this.   The recipient has three entirely different additional worlds of experience, touch, taste and smell. Removing a pip, showing it to the audience, and presenting two or three photographic slides of an apple tree in its developing stages, one explains that from the pip the apple tree grows. For what we call an apple is simply *the fruit*, not only is every stage from the pip through to the tree and on to the next generation of fruit an *apple*, so too, is the role of the earth, water, air and fire (sun) every bit as much, *part of an apple*. All are inseparably united, yet all are individual realities and concepts in their own right, revealing Heraclitus' enigmatic statement, "The logos is both that which is content *and* not content, to be called by the name of Zeus", suddenly crystal clear. We perceive the world in infinite separate percepts, yet it is we alone that can unite them into meaningful content. That which is separate is always united with other entities. There is no indication whatsoever simply by observing through any or all the five senses that the fruit originates from a pip which in turn will develop into a tree which again will bear fruit. If the fruit appears as nothing like the tree to the senses and yet is inseparable from it and part of its reality, what right do we have to assume that the human form is the entirety of the human being? One does not ask anyone to accept anything on authority. It is not a question of belief, but of humility.   One should not assume that because one cannot see anything, that there is not anything to see. To anthroposophical readers, this apparently long-winded example appears obvious, but we should not forget that from consistent experience with listeners both academic and in the commercial world, the above is most certainly *not* obvious. This apparently simple analogy of the apple is indispensable for 'clearing the ground' before we can proceed toward our objective. It creates that magical place outside time and space between speaker and audience where a holy place of silence and higher space exists where human spirits meet upon mutual ground in the common ideal to move from the realm of knowledge into the sphere of wisdom or, more prosaically, 'the open mind'.

The Hero

Upon this hallowed ground we must open up a vision of exactly what we are fighting for: man as a living spirit with the power of the godhead *within* him. That is where mythology and history become a revelation in the hero, or rather, the heroic.

Every one loves a story, every story has a hero. Whether you are a child or the boss of a multi-national company the heroic has the power to raise man to his full stature. The heroic in man is *epic* in our consciousness. Mythology and history are *epic* in the story of man's unfolding. The task remains to reveal the epic within us.

We need to help people realise that we cannot hope to understand anything concerning the tragedies, sufferings, problems, possibilities and potential facing mankind, unless we recognise that the nature of man is epic. That we are epic in our consciousness - being both macrocosmic and microcosmic simultaneously.

To feel that our individual life is absolutely essential and indispensable to the future of the world, regardless of where destiny has placed us, we must be able to recognise that we are part of a vast battle in a long war not against each other but against that which manifests as the relegation of Man's being to that of an animal or, his apparent promotion to the form of an organic machine. The false humility of *'you are only an insignificant speck of dust'*, and the wallowings of *'we are, after all, only animals'* must be swept from the field and replaced by man as individual, potentially free-willed being, deeply responsible to and for his fellows. I have found it ideal when presenting this to others on a professional basis, to show how mankind's vision of itself has metamorphosed over comparatively few millennia.

Looking at the heroes of the Greek and Teutonic peoples, (my most beloved here are my childhood friends, Odysseus and Siegfried) and of how a task was set to them, a journey through many trials (usually twelve) was required before any return either home or to one's eternal bride (hero is to spirit as bride is to soul) was possible. The *nostos* of the Greeks being a return to the same point only after initiation, emerging on a higher level. Each hero was always watched over by a god or goddess, walking beside the one they loved, preparing the hero for his forthcoming trials, yet never undertaking them on his behalf. Athena watches over her beloved Odysseus, Wotan over his Siegfried. Often the hero is angry with his divine helper. Can we not see here the soul kicking against the spirit's infallible wisdom? Desire battling against understanding and conscience? In ancient times these pictures accounted for the stability of the ancient peoples - one need only look at the civilisation of Egypt, (Osiris/Isis myth) or Chaldea (Gilgamesh/Eabani). These peoples were stable because they were not awake - dreaming divine dreams, panoramas - a film, a spiritual movie enthralling them, knowing thereby their place was ensured in the cosmic story. The screenwriters were the Gods - each actor had many parts for he had many lives - everyone had a part. Gradually each actor emerged from the crowd scenes, the chorus, and took on a small speaking part, no matter how insignificant it appeared, upon whatever each actor spoke and how he moved, hung the whole thread of the play. Everyone gradually was given his 'big' moment - his awakening to self-consciousness. Exeunt Odysseus, Siegfried, enter Greek philosophy - the spoken word utters sublime thoughts, the depths of which philosophy we have not even remotely equalled today. Slowly Athena no longer accompanies Odysseus - the one who is so out of kilter with all those around him in both Iliad and Odyssey, whose counsel is sought and admired by all and yet who is feared and mistrusted by all. The archetypal loner. Athena now descends slowly *into* him. From myth to history. The daemon spoken of by Socrates and Plato descends to hover above an ever greater number of individual human beings and we awake standing at the trial of Christ. Zarathustra, Moses, Elijah, Isaiah, Daniel, Zeno, Heraclitus, Socrates, Plato and Aristotle - the spiritual world's 'crack troops' all have borne the torch, guided the daemon of each human being - the *'I am the I am'* closer and closer to become the *'I am **in** the I am'*, so that we stand no longer in the crowd watching Christ, Pilate and the Sanhedrin battle for the Vision of man, but are each of us drawn from the crowd as if in a dream to awake *in* the being of Pilate. This much maligned and misunderstood lofty individuality - lest we forget - was the last human being with whom the Christ ever held conversation on Earth. It was not with Desmas or Gestas (the two thieves), not with John the Divine or the Holy Sophia at the foot of the Cross, for to these He simply gave a summons or made a statement. With Pilate, Christ meets him, He recognises the human spirit struggling through to *recognition* of Him, drawing Pilate ever upward without interfering with his freedom, He forgives his doubt and what is wrongly seen by theologians and historians for 2000 years as lack of moral courage, is not judged as such by Christ. He sheds the clearest light upon the dichotomy between freewill and duty 1,968 years before most of us have been faced with it. Exonerating Pilate for what he needs must do in this cosmic play, He summons the individual to recognise Him, I to I, from God to man, to God in man. Now, the Logos in man sleeps, awaiting the door to be opened *("Behold, I stand at the door and knock")*. St. John the Divine gives us such a picture of the Risen One in man and on towards Spirit man. So on once more from myth to history and to myth again. Parsifal is an archetype for the one who awakens, recognising that he is responsible to and for all his fellows. One who becomes the King of the Grail, because he serves his fellows (St. John 13 particularly vv. 12-17). In history, von Eschenbach gives his archetypal picture that was still understood as the time of confusion sets in (the Mediaeval Era). In history again, Aquinas christens the wisdom of the classical world in time for the birth of Natural Science and the impending battle for the human soul (that for the human spirit having been apparently lost some 400 years earlier at the Council of Constantinople). Now the spoken words of the great mediaeval thinkers Alanus ab Insulis, John Scotus Erigena and even the gritty and martial St. Bernard of Clairvaux, fall quiet, as the written word conquers the spoken.

Martin Luther brings down a fiery sword rending a new veil, that of the Catholic Temple. Particularly from the 15th Century onwards, people hungered for what was written. If it was known more widely just how many people were burned, tortured, flayed and blinded for possession of the written word *Word*, we could more easily recognise that what was once still perceived as a *call* from the Spirit became a feint imprint on a page. And so to the 20th Century. What shape our picture of man now? Whence are we exalted to follow? Which banner are we hailed to rally toward?

It is now the era of the Visual Image. No longer the inner Imagination but the outer image. The Cosmic Movie of the Living Spirit is now cellulosed and digitised. It is externalised, coming to us from without, sending us to sleep as we prostrate ourselves before the Almighty Gods of Stomach and Crotch. Our temples the supermarkets to which daily pilgrimage is made, especially on Sundays. Our altars the cars upon which we heap offerings. And our oracles, the cinemas and television from which we vainly hope for nourishment and guidance, from an endless proliferation of dumb priestesses, exhorting us to 'Know what I want, what I really, *really* want', whilst the soul of man struggles to ask, "What do I *need*, do I really, *really need?* Well then, what do we really, really need? For a start, we recognise that the heroic has become shameful, and the mediocre something 'to aspire to'. That the cosmic film has run its course, the credits are over. For a brief moment we were aware that it was ourselves who were the actors in this Divine Play. Now we need a new screenplay. The problem is, that this one, we have to write ourselves. For this we need imagination, inspiration. If we wish to take the gold from beneath the dragon's wings, we have to enter into the dragon's realm. Take his fire to warm, resuscitate and revive. Metamorphose it from burning, searing and destructive passion into life-giving warmth. As anthroposophists, we turn the enemy's weapon upon himself, not to destroy him but to disarm him, just as Michael does not destroy the dragon, recognising that the visual image is the latest weapon in the army of opposing powers, bludgeoning us towards spiritual annihilation. At a time when we should be awakening Imaginative cognition from within, we are being put to sleep through blinding pictures from without, by images which are thrusting the burning stake into our gently awakening spiritual eye. What Odysseus did to Polyphemus was a sublime image for that which was right and necessary. Now Christ has been and gone and awaits us in His kingdom, this image must be reversed as Christ is to open the eye in WIDE AWAKE CONSCIOUSNESS.

Bearing in mind that the opposition is not our fellow man, but that which finds a way to work through us, I resolved to present the heroic, the epic in us, as the one picture that can approach us from the outside, through the world of film, whilst awakening us from within. Enter the Hero.

In all films, there is a hero figure, regardless of how the heroic manifests. It may be a Terminator, a Luke Skywalker, a Disney Hercules, a Jack Dawson (Titanic), or a 'talented' Mr. Ripley. Nevertheless, people long for a hero - one who overcomes great odds to achieve something for himself, and the helpless, hapless hordes who await their redemption through him. The fact that none of the above ever existed, is another worrying issue. Firstly, the hero is the one who only comes through to take the girl (Titanic). Personal salvation of only that which concerns me and mine, otherwise 'every man for himself'! Or our hero can be a destroyer - a Luke Skywalker and his friends. Hand in hand with this, and especially for the very young, heroic qualities in the animal - The Lion King - how can an animal ever possess heroic qualities, I hear you ask? Well, if you want a picture of man as noble animal, give the animal a name and personality, and get it into the very young human as a picture as soon as you can (Disney Productions). Simultaneously, for the adolescent, take divine spiritual truths - The Ark of the Covenant, The Holy Grail, etc. and externalise them to such a degree that the physical symbol takes on mystical powers as an earthly object, sought by corduroy clad archaelogists and closet Nazis. For the childish adolescents and adults, as opposed to the childlike, enter science fiction. Invent illusory heroes to fight imaginary enemies from impossible realms, and we have the X Files, Star Wars, The Terminator, where the flawed and frightened humans are rescued by the self-sacrificing moral machine (incidentally it is my belief that the Terminator films are worth much meditation for they are far deeper than one at first becomes aware of. The evil and redemptive are shown in a manner that is constantly metamorphosing and thus demanding extraordinary vigilance). So, expressed succinctly, on the one hand the animal becomes human, and on the other, the human becomes machine.

The above is, in very condensed form, the picture I endeavour to paint of the vast sweep of human consciousness as it has metamorphosed and evolved. A picture that is perceivable to those working in education, the arts, commerce and industry, who have no knowledge of anthroposophy, in order to awaken a vision of the dignity and potential of man in Christ's words, "Ye are Gods" and yet simultaneously of "How the mighty are fallen". A picture that inspires a question from the listener.

A Film of the Battle Of Trafalgar

Having realised that mythology cannot be presented on film in such a direct manner as even thirty years ago, one must clothe it in new apparel. The screenplay for Parsifal has been written and in such a form as to present karmic responsibility and reincarnation as a reality, by moving the story between two different eras, allowing for both the magical and historical element to be presented in a manner that will lead the audience out of its familiar parameters of time and space unambiguously from the Old Testament concept of reciprocity and replacing it with remembrance, recognition and responsibility, leading to the New Testament spirit - forgiveness.

Reincarnation and karma cannot be approached and presented to an audience by the medium of cinema, if people are not encouraged to understand that responsibility to and for others was very much a part of life up until a few decades ago, as opposed to much talk of it being evident today, and evidence of deed largely absent. Here the concept of duty is something very different from that of following orders. Again, the question of free will and necessity looms. Walking to the International Festival of the

Sea in Portsmouth, in August 1998, pondering the question, "How can we approach the heroic in film?", it was clear that mythology would leave people feeling, "Yes, wonderful, but it's just myth, isn't it?" As I entered the Historic Dockyard I turned at best semi-consciously into a huge hangar, and there, suspended and towering above many onlookers was the awe-inspiring sight of the only remaining sail from H.M.S. Victory (the main foretopsail) recently discovered in a sail loft in the dockyard, having been stored some two centuries earlier after Victory returned triumphant from Trafalgar in 1805. Hung for the first time since it was taken down during the battle, the shot holes and scorch marks were strikingly evident. At forty years of age I stood before it in complete awe and cried. *There* was the heroic in history. There had never been a film about Trafalgar - Nelson, yes, but never Trafalgar. For the next ten months, I practically lived between the Admiralty Libraries and the Public Records Office, researching the original muster and log books from all 27 British ships which fought at Trafalgar and from the 33 Spanish and French ships, together with hundreds of first-hand accounts left to us by men of all ranks and nations who fought. Piecing together the battle and recognising that men from over twenty different nations were fighting in the Royal Navy and men from at least ten different nations were fighting in the Franco-Spanish Combined Fleet, it became clear that as early as 1805, souls were fighting for a vision of Europe and not for patriotism alone. That Horatio Nelson - born incidentally on the 29th September 1758 - was a deeply religious and humane man, loved for his ability to reach right to the ' I ' of each one, regardless of race, rank or nation, in a time when hierarchy was far more pronounced than it is today, a picture began to unfold of men such as Collingwood, Hardy, Duff, Cooke and Villeneuve, Gravina, Lucas and Cherucca, and not only the captains, but also the thousands from the lower decks who all lived by a totally different moral standard, personally courageous almost beyond our comprehension. The ideals of courage, sacrifice, devotion and love shone through so powerfully, and the concepts of torture, massacre and war crimes so totally alien to their consciousness, that we justifiably present a convincing case for questioning exactly when *are* the Dark Ages. The time in which they lived was physically harsh but it drew from them truly human qualities. In studying Nelson's prayer penned on the morning of Trafalgar as the two British columns approached the Franco-Spanish line about to commence the most decisive naval battle in history, it was clear that here were men wrapped inevitably in the karma of their era, their nations and their personal karma, but who consciously gave themselves over to a higher will in complete spiritual freedom. All the captains who fought at Trafalgar were deeply religious men, giving themselves with complete commitment and faith to whatever the day would bring and to the struggle for a vision of man and of the future Europe. The scope of this article will not allow for an adequate picture of just how remarkable these individuals and events were. It must be left to the forthcoming film to do them justice.

It became clear to me that two words should be obliterated from human comprehension - 'coincidence' and 'compromise'. Anyone who aspires to represent or portray historical truths, exoteric or esoteric, is bound by an inner law - that of moral historical responsibility, and karmically unites himself with whatever consequences his work engenders. This is the founding impulse behind the planned films. That this is not generally acknowledged, let alone embraced, is the cause of endless suffering and heaps much bitter destiny to follow upon mankind.

In all areas of pre-production the screenplay has been met with a remarkable sense of recognition of both the theme, the form and the spirit in which it is written. Such diverse bodies as The Royal Navy, Royal Marines, City of Portsmouth, National Maritime Museum, St. Paul's Cathedral, the authorities in Gibraltar, Antigua, Spain and France and two multi-national companies have already pledged their support to this endeavour, together with considerable contributions from within the film industry and the City.

The first humble step in reaching our fellow men, regardless of where destiny has placed them, and whatever world picture they bear, is to present them with a 'better film' than the one they are watching. Firstly, that man is not an animal; secondly, that he is not a machine. 7000 years of even only recorded history testifies to something greater and far nobler than that. If we approach the so called 'halls of power' through Art, we need not fear the medium we use, provided we are awake to the content and aware of the impulse from which our work arises. Often the most unlikely and influential of individuals are seeking for a new manner of understanding with which to ally their considerable earthly achievements A third of the way through the Michaelic era, we should feel confident to hack furiously through the Gordian Knot. There is a desperate hunger and surprising openness coming to meet us, which makes one realise that by now, there should hardly be anyone on earth who has not heard of anthroposophy and a majority should have had the opportunity of exposure to at least one of its impulses and have experienced its first fruits. There is gold under the dragon's wings and it is time to take it, use it and return it to where it belongs. Trafalgar is a major feature film due for release in 2004, ahead of the bicentenary of the battle.

Ending with Nelson's prayer, the reader may meditate upon the content offered up by this most Michaelic of souls. Suffice it to say that, one of the most remarkable things concerning the Battle of Trafalgar and the events that followed, was not only that it changed the course of European and world history, but that all the petitions were entirely and uncompromisingly granted in the highest degree.

> *May the Great God, whom I worship,*
> *Grant to my Country, and for the benefit of Europe in general*
> *A great and glorious Victory;*
> *And may no misconduct in anyone tarnish it;*
> *And may humanity after Victory, be the predominant feature in*
> *the British Fleet.*
> *For myself, individually, I commit my life to Him who made me,*
> *And may His blessing light upon my endeavours for serving my*
> *Country faithfully.*
> *To Him I resign myself and the just cause which is entrusted to*
> *me to defend.*
> *Amen. Amen. Amen.*

Post Script: "Ready! Aye Ready!" was the response of each of the gun crews on a British Man of War ship awaiting battle, as the question "Ready?" was shouted down the decks by their captains. It is both the summons and answer most appropriate to us in the Michaelic era.

Book Review

The Encounter with Evil and its Overcoming through Spiritual Science by Sergei O. Prokofieff

By Nicholas Nunhofer

It is something of an anthroposophical truism to say that this is the age of materialism. That this is also the age of evil - in the same way as the time of the Enlightenment is called the age of reason - would be a far harder statement for many anthroposophists to swallow. And yet a dispassionate assessment of the enormous crimes of the last century - state sponsored genocide on a wholly unprecedented scale, two world wars immediately followed by the balance of terror of the Cold War - show that the forces of evil have made considerable progress in their efforts to gain a stranglehold over human development

The spiritual science of anthroposophy that Rudolf Steiner developed in the first quarter of the twentieth century adds immeasurably to humanity's knowledge, and hence understanding, of evil. The first, and longest, essay of this book is based on two lectures given by the author to mark the year 1998 as the third re-occurrence of the number of the beast (666) in outer history. Drawing on the full extent of Steiner's corpus it contains many fascinating insights into the workings of evil, especially during the twentieth century. It also looks ahead to the immanent incarnation of the Anti-Christ, Ahriman/Satan.

According to the author, the seductive power of this incarnation will be so immense that practically all of the part of earthly humanity (which today is the overwhelming majority) who are immersed in the contemporary exoteric culture will succumb. Only those communities and groups of individuals who have anchored themselves in the Christ-filled world of the etheric (where the Second Coming is now taking place) will be able to withstand the seductive power of this incarnation.

It was to this end that Rudolf Steiner (who proclaimed the Second Coming of Christ after it began in the Spiritual World after 1909) gave the Foundation Stone of the Good to the newly formed Anthroposophical

Society at the Christmas Conference of 1923/24. Formed and fashioned entirely out of the wide etheric expanses of the cosmos this Foundation Stone will, if taken up and carried with sufficient earnestness by anthroposophists, be the guarantor for the Anthroposophical Society that it to does not succumb to the all-embracing power of Ahriman as he enters into incarnation at the beginning of this millennium.

It is for this purpose that this volume includes, as its last essay, the great lecture given by the author in Great Britain in 1990 entitled: *The path to a Spiritual Experience of Christ; the Appearance of Christ in Etheric form and the Essential Nature of the Foundation Stone of the Christmas Conference.*

Of particular interest to the reviewer was the elucidation given in the book of the four streams of goodness that have sought to further the progress of Christianity since the Mystery of Golgotha. They are the Grail stream, the Manichean impulse, the Knights Templar and the Rosicrucians. The reviewer found that thinking of these streams in relation to one's own karma and that of ones fellow anthroposophical acquaintances proved most fruitful.

This slender volume (in comparison with some of the author's other works) is a rich fund of highly relevant knowledge to help make the new century not an even worse nightmare than its predecessor in many respects was.

Book Review

Awakening the Will
and
Practising Destiny

by Coenraad van Houten
Temple Lodge Publishing, London (1999 & 2000)

Awakening The Will

At the dawn of a new millennium, formal education is more widely available than ever before in the history of humanity and at the same time is increasingly widely in question: what are the appropriate aims, purposes, methods etc. in each given location. There are inner and outer pressures which sharpen the debate. In a fast-moving global economy, job security is a thing of the past, and education is required to help people meet the changing demands of the work-place, whether in or out of work. On the other hand, as society becomes increasingly differentiated, and geared to the demands of the individual, with leisure, whether voluntary or involuntary, more and more available, people experience the need to go beyond what they have received from the home or school by way of culture, and to pursue and develop interests arising from inner needs. These two books by Coen van Houten are aimed at those providing and receiving adult education, and draw on his many years of experience as an adult educator.

The key questions addressed are: How do we actually learn? What obstacles do we meet? How do we deal with them? Drawing on Rudolf Steiner's lecture series entitled "The Riddle of Humanity" (Rudolf Steiner Press 1990), Coen van Houten describes the seven life processes which ebb and flow within the cosmos of our twelve senses. These are seven activities of the etheric, or life- body which, as we know from Steiner's lectures on education, is primarily occupied with building up the physical body until the change of teeth around the age of 6-7 years, and then becomes partially free to provide us with the faculties which we need in order to be educated.

Van Houten's premise is: given that it is the etheric body which is the prime vehicle for learning, its seven main activities are an archetype for the process of learning itself. Thus all learning involves the equivalent of breathing, warming, nourishing, secreting, maintaining, growing and reproducing. It is clearly a premise which he has tested extensively during his years in adult education, and in consequence presents very convincingly, with many practical examples.

Thought has been given to a wide range of practical considerations - working with colleagues, appropriate hygiene in the structure of a course, effective use of time, using a course diary etc. There are also guidelines on group work and useful appendices by others who have applied this principle in particular areas of study.

The book is not one which one would readily read from cover to cover, (it has been generally well translated from German, but there are occasional awkward moments) and it does, as Van Houten freely admits in the introduction, contain some passages which are less developed than others, but is nevertheless very well organised, so that one can find one's way quickly to the parts that may be relevant to a particular question one might have. My impression is that it could well become a very valuable reference work for anyone running a course of whatever length on whatever subject.

Practising Destiny

Anyone embarking on a course of study will soon find that part of the process involves getting to know oneself better - one's strengths and weaknesses, but also the behaviour patterns that manifest in relationships, trends which become apparent in one's biography etc. This is clearly unique to each individual , as are the character and timing of the "lucky breaks" and "blows of fate" that befall one. Careful observation can lead to the development of a sense of destiny, a sense that there are particular life tasks belonging to each individual.

In this second volume on principles and processes in adult learning, Coen van Houten applies the learning archetype to this "destiny learning", showing how, whilst it may seem to be an entirely individual concern, the process may be enhanced by consciously working together with others with whom one has a shared destiny and how this may therefore have considerable social benefits.

This work is clearly still in its infancy and has a strongly experimental character. It is therefore particularly helpful that the book includes a series of articles by people who have worked in various settings, including management consultancy, art therapy and biography work. There is also a very stimulating essay by Lex Bos on the dynamics of judgement forming, which I can recommend to anyone who has to try to work productively in meetings.

The focus of destiny learning is on everyday incidents with other people, enhancing one's observation of them, and learning to see through the phenomena to the destiny forces at work behind them. It follows that there is a need to develop techniques of encounter which enable one to penetrate through the obstacles of convention, habit, prejudice etc. There are two good passages on this, the second by Shirley Routledge. As Coen van Houten puts it: "In order to remain within the process of encounter one must continuously bring one's ego into a rhythmical alternation between establishing oneself and opening oneself to the other".

This work is still at such an early stage in its development that it is probably too early to judge the effectiveness of the techniques put forward in "Practising Destiny" - time will tell, but those who have a question leading in this direction will find in this book informed and experienced guidance that is accessible and clear.

W.B Forward

Letter to the Editors

In the 2000 edition of the Golden Blade, Enge, Smit and Schage, three Norwegian doctors whom I shall refer to as "the authors", comment on two articles by Jostein Saether published in Norway. In their notes, the editors indicate that this is intended as a response to an article by Saether published in the 1998 edition. When I read their article, I confess that my first reaction was indignation. I paused, in fact for several months, while I considered this. However, having given it the measure of time I still fear that, as published, it may constitute an unfair treatment of Saether on five counts and I should like to explain these.

1. This is edited material with uncertain claims

My first concern is that this article is out of context. It is not a response to the original Golden Blade piece, which would have been valuable. Instead, the authors respond to and criticise two articles by Saether published in Norway in Norwegian, meaning that most readers have to rely on the authors' descriptions of Saether's content. Part of the article, dealing with Saether's approach to Rudolf Steiner's source material, has been cut, leaving us unable to assess the background of either party's approach to Steiner's original karma research proposals. I cannot judge the value of the article in its original context, but as it stands, I feel uneasy.

This unease increases as I find a number of differences between what I understand Saether to have been saying in the Golden Blade in 1998 and what the authors argue that he is saying in the Norwegian article. For example, they make a point of Saether's remark that, "Astonishingly good results have come through", and that "one can reckon on quick results". However, in 1998, Saether reports that his first experience took place 25 years earlier and that since that time and before his present public claims he studied intensively in a number of fields of life and anthroposophy. He describes life crises and then a process of working intensely and virtually every day on karma research without results. Then he says, "one day it happened suddenly that my inner sight was awakened." This is of course exactly how Steiner indicates in Knowledge of the Higher Worlds that breakthroughs happen. My impression is that the authors are objecting to claims to be able to help others achieve results that they think Saether makes. Yet, we are not privy to knowing exactly what they are objecting to, only that they find it objectionable. The authors also claim that he lacks humility and critical evaluation. Yet, we are not provided with any evidence of this. His remarks in the Golden Blade are modest: "Until other researchers come to similar or conflicting results which can be used to verify or contradict what is set out below, I shall consider my research and references to past incarnations as *possible assumptions with some degree of probability"*. Is Saether's work being drawn into disrepute without a fair trial?

2. There was no opportunity for Saether to reply
I would very much appreciate a sound evaluation of Saether's work and a good discussion of karma research. I expect that Saether would appreciate this too. In that respect, I congratulate the editors for airing the subject. To enable this, I believe it would have been reasonable in these circumstances if Saether had had an opportunity to reply.

3. Possible misrepresentation through misunderstanding?
My third area of concern is that I believe the authors may sometimes misunderstand Steiner and Saether. Let me give you examples.

They protest that Saether has "Imaginations" and perceives pictures in "clear outlines" in his spiritual experiences. They argue that karmic research is based on Intuition (i.e. not in Imagination and pictures) and that only this permits research into repeated lives on Earth. However, Steiner makes many different statements including the observation that spiritual knowledge is paradoxical. Their opinion is based on one statement by Steiner in Occult Science: "Anything which purports to be the truth *about these processes* must stem from research by means of Intuitive faculties". However, Steiner is here describing how to research the *processes* of karma and repeated lives and not the personal *experience* of karma and past lives. In Karmic Relationships volume II, we find a number of Steiner's most explicit descriptions of how to do karma research and I believe these present a different idea. In the lecture of 27th of April 1924, he describes, as part of an introduction to the studies in karma, the need to grasp hold of inner reality in imaginations and pictures. In the next lecture (of 4th May 1924), he described how the karma researcher must see through outer phenomena in a person's gestures and appearance so that a picture appears. He explained, "...as long as I merely see this fact, the picking up of the chalk, then I know nothing of karma. I must do away with all this. I must bring it about that all this can reproduce itself in a *picture*, can appear again in a *picture"* (my italics). Finally, in the next lecture of 9th of May 1924, he went into great detail on how to elaborate a picture that illuminates past lives. This seems to me to be a clear reference to Imaginative consciousness.

As a second example of possible misunderstanding, the authors claim that they find a lack of awareness of the guardian of the threshold in Saether's work. I cannot comment on the Norwegian article, but if that is the case, I would recommend them to the Golden Blade article. There, Saether makes a number of comments that clearly deal with this being, although he does not use this term. Instead, he approaches the subject first in relationship to the double, then through Christ as the Lord of Karma and finally through the need to work with one's own unredeemed evil. In that respect, it seems to me that he helps to elucidate the manifold nature of the "guardian of the threshold". From personal conversation with Saether, it is my impression that these are highly significant to him.

On such points, a response from Saether might also have been helpful.

4. Karma is not simply an individual affair

My fourth subject of concern touches an important and, to be fair to the authors, probably controversial subject. Apparently, Saether suggests that it is appropriate, in certain circumstances, to be "radically intimate" in revealing information about contemporaries and, furthermore, to use knowledge gained about another person's past lives without asking for his or her approval. Assuming this reflects Saether's intentions, then I think he raises an important question that deserves considerable discussion. I am familiar with and sensitive to the idea that our past karma is our own, private affair. However, It appears to me that there may *in principle* be no difference between revealing something about a past life and revealing something from earlier in a present life. My past lives are *at least* as influential as my childhood in shaping who I am. Which of us has not tried to explain the behaviour of someone we know to another upset friend by revealing how this behaviour arose from some earlier, perhaps childhood, experience? I imagine that every one of us has depended on our parents reminding us about incidents in our childhood life that we do not remember. The issue, it seems to me is, at least in part, the degree to which such revelation is accurate and the motive in so doing. One can spread slander about a contemporary or one can seek to enable others to understand and appreciate him or her better. It is a question of tact, discretion, reliability and respect. In a world in which we do not know about other people's past lives, nor indeed about our own, to spread information about their supposed past lives could only be fabrication and rumour. However, how do things become when we start to have some real certainty about past lives? Should we not, as the modern age of spiritual science develops, begin to assume that such certainty is possible? What are the ethical consequences of this?

In talking about a person's present life, it will sometimes not be appropriate to reveal what we know. Instead, we might need to say something like, "I think there are things about that person's life that you might need to ask about before you form a judgement". On another occasion, it will be appropriate to say what we know. It seems to me that, in principle, much the same things apply when working with reliable research into past lives. Furthermore, one might assume that an ethically sound researcher might also develop not only the right judgement as to when this is appropriate, but also might have access to sources of guidance from across the threshold. As karma and past life knowledge become, more and more, accepted fact, I suggest we will need to become more and more skilled in offering and receiving such advice. In other words, each of us may need to develop not only appropriate skills in giving information about past lives, but also skills in asking for and receiving such information. If we are to create truly healthy, social relationships in an increasingly egocentric world, I suspect we will have little choice. For, karma is surely not simply an individual affair! I need to understand my own past if I am to become fully, socially responsible. I can, for example, indicate that a discovery in one of my own past lives has helped me to improve a behaviour that others have found offensive for many years. It has also helped me to make sense of and to find freedom from a bitter karmic knot. If we are to develop love and, eventually, overcome the war of all against all, do we not need to understand past life relationships with each other? Far from being just my own affair, karma is surely an intensely inter-dependent, social concern.

5. Are we encouraging karma research?

My final concern goes to what may be the heart of the matter: the issue of revelation of past lives. The authors appear to believe that it is inappropriate for a spiritual researcher to reveal knowledge of his or her own past lives. They find Saether immodest in quoting the apparent results of his research and believe that he is in conflict with classic esoteric practice. In our present time, I am not sure that one can judge the modesty or otherwise of a human soul from such an abstract principle. I do not believe that we should consider that it is appropriate to discuss the theory but not at all appropriate to discuss the practice of spiritual research. I have the impression that Saether seeks to breathe new life and commitment into Anthroposophical karma research, an activity fundamental to Rudolf Steiner's work and aims, and, I believe, to the needs of contemporary society. I think, from a conversation with Saether, that this is what lies behind his "coming out" with the results of his research. Putting oneself in a position to attract criticism can be a painful experience and a sacrifice. The world advances through innovation, the test for which is found in its consequences. In order that we do not discourage the sharing of spiritual-scientific research, let us deal with those who do come forward in an open and fair way, assessing what they bring from a human and not an abstract perspective. As has been widely documented, Steiner was prevented from developing karma research once in his lifetime due to the reaction of his contemporaries. Let us neither blindly accept what others say, nor be so biased in mood or practice that we prevent our contemporaries from developing and sharing their research.

Angus Jenkinson

Notes on the Contributors

Corinna Gleide (born 1964) works in Munich, with the Gesellschaft für Ausbildungsforschung und Berufsentwicklung (GAB). She gives anthroposophical courses on a freelance basis in Heidelberg.

Sergei Prokofieff (born 1954 in Moscow) writes and lectures on anthroposophical themes. He was a co-founder of the Anthroposophical Society in Russia (1990) and is currently its representative in Dornach. He lives in Germany.

Harlan Gilbert is from the USA and trained and practised as an architect. Following teacher training at Emerson College, he taught for several years at Wynstones School.

Jonael Schickler studied philosophy at Cambridge and is currently engaged in post-graduate work there.

Bodo von Plato (born 1958 in Bad Bevensen, Germany) has been involved since 1989 in the development and leadership of the Forschungstelle Kulturimpuls at the Friedrich von Hardenberg Institute for Cultural Sciences in Heidelberg.

Bernard Jarman is at present Executive Director of the Bio-Dynamic Agricultural Association. After himself farming at Botton Village, he served for several years on the Council of the BDAA, including five years as its Chairman (1995-2000).

James Dyson MD practises medicine and is currently a director of the Park Attwood Clinic in Stourbridge.

Alex Naylor has worked with the Mary Rose Trust in Portsmouth and teaches and lectures in Russian and on Mythology.